LUDWIG ALSDORF AND INDIAN STUDIES

Ludwig Alsdorf.

LUDWIG ALSDORF
AND
INDIAN STUDIES

Edited by
Klaus Bruhn
Magdalene Duckwitz
Albrecht Wezler

MOTILAL BANARSIDASS PUBLISHERS
PRIVATE LIMITED
DELHI

First Edition: Delhi, 1990

ISBN: 81-208-0681-6

Also available at:
MOTILAL BANARSIDASS
Bungalow Road, Jawahar Nagar, Delhi 110 007
Chowk, Varanasi 221 001
Ashok Rajpath, Patna 800 004
24 Race Course Road, Bangalore 560 001
120 Royapettah High Road, Mylapore, Madras 600 004

PRINTED IN INDIA
BY JAINENDRA PRAKASH JAIN AT SHRI JAINENDRA PRESS, A-45 NARAINA INDUSTRIAL AREA, PHASE I, NEW DELHI 110028 AND PUBLISHED BY NARENDRA PRAKASH JAIN FOR MOTILAL BANARSIDASS PUBLISHERS PVT. LTD., BUNGALOW ROAD, JAWAHAR NAGAR, DELHI 110007.

TABLE OF CONTENTS

EDITORS' NOTE

LUDWIG ALSDORF (1904-1978) was one of the most active and competent exponents of recent German Indology. He has made lasting contributions to various branches of Indian studies—we mention only Jainism, Buddhism and Veda. But he has also studied and described Indian history and civilization as a whole. The greater part of his writings is meant for the specialist. But he was also fully aware of the need to inform a wider public. L. Alsdorf's researches are deeply rooted in the tradition of German scholarship but he was too original a thinker to conform to any established pattern. His range of interests was wide and his activities were manifold.

The numerous articles and reviews from his pen had been published in a great number of European and Indian journals. In order to bring this material together, his collected articles were published in 1974 on the occasion of his 70th birthday. This was to be followed by a Felicitation Volume published five years later and presented to him on his 75th birthday. L. Alsdorf's unexpected death in 1978 made it necessary to change these plans. As a consequence, a Commemoration Volume was published in 1981, three years after his death.*

The concept of this brochure originated in the course of the work on that volume. The basic idea was to give broad information on all the aspects of L. Alsdorf's work both to the learned general public and to co-specialists who had no adequate access to his own writings. Under the circumstances, the present booklet could not be quite uniform in all its parts. Furthermore, it shows here and there the traits of an experiment. The editors are nevertheless confident that it will help to focus attention on a great scholar and at the same time encourage later Indologists to utilize L. Alsdorf's writings to their fullest possible extent.

**Studien zum Jainismus und Buddhismus—Gedenkschrift für Ludwig Alsdorf*
Ed. by Klaus Bruhn & Albrecht Wezler,
Alt - und Neuindische Studien 23 (University of Hamburg), Franz Steiner Verlag GmbH, Wiesbaden 1981

The publication is a digest which consists of several parts different in character and contributed by various scholars. For a number of reasons it proved necessary to supply for most chapters additional informations of one type or the other which might have been presented as foot-notes, prolegomena, etc. It seemed, however, simpler to collect this material in the "Editors' Note" instead of providing the various parts with supplements of differing character.

(1) The Obituary on pp. 5-13 is the revised English version of the original German text (*Zeitschrift der Deutschen Morgenländischen Gesellschaft* [Journal of the German Oriental Society], Vol. 129. 1979, pp. 1-7). Basically it is a "reprint", and not an article specially written for the present publication. We have to add, that work on the *Critical Pāli Dictionary* is being continued: fascicle II 10 was published after Alsdorf's death, still carrying his name. Fascicles II 11-12 (*uparima-uposathakiriyā uposathakumāra-uḷumpa*) have been published since then and 13 is under preparation. The Editor-in-Chief for fasc. II 11 foll. is K.R. Norman. The obituary included in II 11 (also by K.R. Norman) describes in detail Alsdorf's work for the *Critical Pāli Dictionary*.

(2) The Bibliography on pp. 15-31 is mainly a reprint (pp. V foll.) from *Ludwig Alsdorf, Kleine Schriften* ed. by A. Wezler (= *Glasenapp-Stiftung* Vol. 10, Franz Steiner Verlag GmbH, Wiesbaden 1974). As far as this was technically possible, we have replaced the German captions by their English equivalents. Two supplements have been added under Nos. IV and V. For the purpose of easier referencing we have provided the titles with numbers running from 1 up to 161. These numbers have been used extensively for the sake of reference in our digest ("Bibl. No. 1" etc.). Books etc. edited by Alsdorf — sometimes with considerable sacrifices of time and energy — have been left unnumbered. The page numbers of the *Kleine Schriften* (e.g. "S.464" in the case of Bibl. No. 11), indicating inclusion into the original volume, have been retained.

(3) The Chronology on pp. 33-34 shows the distribution of Alsdorf's writings over the full period of his academic activity (1928 – 1978). We have made a formal distinction between original contributions (standing first) and reviews (added at the end). For reasons which require no explanation we have included

here and in the two following parts (Bibliography of Reviews, Reviews Reprinted) *Varuṇa I-II* and *Critical Pāli Dictionary II* 5-10—two instances of editorial activity—into the survey. The Chronology can also be used in order to identify incomplete references to Alsdorf's writings (provided the reference contains the year). However, the Chronology invariably mentions the year of publication which may be later than the year quoted in a reference (e.g. compare Bibl. No. 14).

(4) The Bibliography of Reviews on pp. 35-44 helps to trace criticisms but also gives an idea of the influence Alsdorf's writings had. Before the fifties, reviews appeared mainly in German language. Later on reviewing was international.

Alsdorf's more general publications appeared under rather different conditions during and after World War II. We are referring mainly to *Indien* (1940), *Deutsch-indische Geistesbeziehungen* (1942), *Indien und Ceylon* (1943), *Vorderindien* (1955), and to his contribution for the *Geschichte Asiens* (1950, Bibl. No. 55). For the Nazis, India had both theoretical and practical importance: Nazi ideologists had adopted the myth of the Aryan race, and political circles attached importance to the opposition against British rule under Subhas Chandra Bose (see p. 6). As a consequence, there was a need for information about India, and Alsdorf's publications filled this gap. His book *Indien* was even translated into Italian (Bibl. No. 51), Italy then being Germany's closest ally. Alsdorf's publications were widely reviewed in contemporary journal literature. But neither did Alsdorf make any concessions to the ideology of the Third Reich nor were all the reviews very political. Much of the reviewing was routine work in the form of short summaries and glosses. All this was possible because Alsdorf was needed as a specialist and because his writings reflected an element of nationalism (as it was not uncommon in those days even amongst the critics of the regime) which can be described in his case as a combination of German and Indian nationalism. Alsdorf took pride in Germany's contributions to Indology and he felt that India should become a free nation with Hindi as its national language. Under the circumstances, some scope was left to discuss even political subjects in a normal manner.———After the end of World War II, the international scene changed radically and in the new context experts for Third World countries were needed more than ever. Besides, there was a growing demand in Germany and elsewhere for better contacts between the specialist and the public. Alsdorf was (in the field of Oriental Studies) one of the few academic teachers in Germany who left the ivory-tower of purely scholarly activities, both by way of his writings and by public lectures. As a consequence, the response to his activities, as reflected in journals, was very positive. It must be added that his book *Vorderindien* also evoked academic criticism and discussion as can be seen in the list and in the two reprints (pp. 51-53 and pp.81-82).

The Bibliography of Reviews also calls for a few technical explations. Reviews have been traced for all independent publications, viz. Bibl. Nos. 1-14 (except Nos. 5 & 8). Apart from this section, R.P. Das has considered Bibl. No. 55 and the two projects mentioned already (*Varuṇa* 1-2 and *Critical Pāli Dictionary*). No. 55 is only a part of the relevant volume *Geschichte Asiens* (History of Asia), and therefore the reviews of this volume should not be expected to dwell upon Alsdorf's essay. By contrast, reviews of other collective publications (felicitation volumes, etc.) have not been included. Let us, therefore, add at this place that Alsdorf answered one such review in his writings. J. Nobel had criticized Alsdorf's paper Bibl. No. 48 in his review of the Winternitz Felicitation Volume of which it formed a part (J. Nobel, *Deutsche Literaturzeitung* 1936, S. 1129-30). Alsdorf not only referred to this critical remark in his *Apabhraṃśa-Studien* (Bibl.No.3), in fact—to quote A. Mette—these studies were partially conceived as an answer to Nobel's criticism (p. 88). —— In the case of *Vorderindien* (Bibl. No.9) the Bibliography of Reviews is based mostly on material collected by the publisher and kindly lent to R.P. Das by Mrs. Mechthild Alsdorf (Göttingen). A few clippings could not be identified and a few notes (meant for private use in libraries but not for publication) have not been listed. —— Needless to add that a bibliography like this — even if prepared with utmost care —can never claim to be quite complete. It must also be mentioned that "review" is a formal definition. Much criticism, often very competent, occurs outside the traditional reviews. —— An asterisk before the title indicates that a review has been reprinted in the present digest. Whenever reprints have been published elsewhere (e.g. H. Lommel on *Varuṇa I*) we have put the asterisk in parentheses.

(5) The Reviews reprinted on pp. 45-82 (see the list in the Table

of Contents) were selected on the basis of the Bibliography prepared by R.P. Das. In the case of three scholars (C. Caillat, J.W. de Jong, K.R. Norman) we have reprinted reviews covering two of Alsdorf's publications. In a number of cases the English reviews were so short that we had to select, for fuller information, French and German reviews. In the case of O. von Hinüber's review of *Critical Pāli Dictionary II 6-10* we have only included the introductory portion but not the long list of observations on individual articles (from *āhaṭanāpaññatti* up to *uparidhāre*). One review (J.W. de Jong on Bibl. Nos. 13-14) has been reprinted for a second time, and Bibl. No. 13 has been considered twice (C. Caillat: Nos. 13/12; J.W. de Jong: 13-14).

(6) A photograph showing Alsdorf in his later years has been published along with the obituaries in *Zeitschr. d. Dtsch. Morgenland. Ges.* 1979 and *Critical Pāli Dictionary II 11*. Our frontispiece shows Alsdorf in earlier years (by courtesy of the *Österreichische Akademie der Wissenschaften* [Austrian Academy of Sciences]). The photograph between pp. 4 and 5 (by courtesy of Mechthild Alsdorf) recalls past days. We see Alsdorf together with Prof. Jetly and Muni Punyavijaya on his second visit to Jaisalmer in 1951. Alsdorf had seen many parts of India but the medieval beauty of the city in the desert with its rich collections of Jaina manuscripts was amongst his most lasting impressions.

* * * * *

The technical details given above shall be supplemented by a few general observations on the form of Alsdorf's writings.

Alsdorf had an excellent command of the English language but did not use it very extensively. Although in his main field of specialization, viz. Jainology, English is more widely used than in other branches of Indology, he never made it a point to write his Jainological contributions exclusively in English. Two of his last articles (Bibl. Nos. 158 and 161), both connected with Jaina literature, were written in German language. His survey of Jainological studies (Bibl. No. 13)—a series of lectures delivered in Paris at the *Collège de France*—was published in French. All this has created problems as far as the promulgation of Alsdorf's researches is concerned. The most satisfactory solution would be translations, summaries or extensive reviews in English language (or in Indian languages) making the German writings as well as the Paris lectures accessible to a wider public. But at this stage such material does not exist in appreciable quantity.

Besides, language is not the only problem. Alsdorf's style was brilliant (see for example the witty survey of previous research in Bibl. No. 18), but even then it is not always easy to follow. Not only did he work on a great variety of subjects, including even Indian mathematics (Bibl. No. 59) and — in the form of a note — Indian music (pp. 436-37 of Bibl. No. 2), he very often included into one and the same contribution observations which are relevant to quite different fields (thus Bibl. No. 18 follows up a problem through Vedic, Buddhist and Jaina literature). Again it is no exaggeration to say that some of his foot-notes are unwritten articles and some of his articles unwritten monographic studies. As a researcher, Alsdorf was restless and even impatient. It can, therefore, not be expected that he shunned risks in his statements and that he hesitated to send a fresh manuscript to the publisher. He knew that his findings would not be in each case the last word, but he probably felt that a mere suggestion could be stimulating if a new problem was tackled.

IN MEMORIAM PROF. DR. LUDWIG ALSDORF

Condolence Meeting on April 17th, 1978 at the Max Müller Bhavan, New Delhi

TO MOURN the death of Prof. Dr. Ludwig Alsdorf, a Condolence Meeting was held at the Max Müller Bhavan, New Delhi. The gathering was attended by the Ambassador of the Federal Republic of Germany, members of the German community and numerous Indian scholars and friends. Among the many tributes paid to the great German savant were the following personal reminiscences of her late teacher by Magdalene Duckwitz:

Friends,

Among those who have assembled here today to commemorate Professor Ludwig Alsdorf it is probably me who has been associated with him longest, first as his student and later as a friend.

I sat at his feet when in 1943, he headed the Department of Indian Studies at Berlin University's short-lived Faculty for the Study of Foreign Relations. His introduction into the phenomena of modern India against the background of her ancient culture made a deep impression on me. Already in these early years when Prof. Alsdorf was not even forty, the tremendous span of his academic occupation with India which singled him out among German and Western Indologists was quite evident. I knew practically nothing then of the region I had chosen to study. But it did not take Prof. Alsdorf long to get me deeply involved in everything Indian. So much so that after the Seminar members had dispersed and fled Berlin under the onslaught of the war in 1945, I continued my Indian studies and also my search for my erstwhile Guru. Under the post-war conditions it took me some time until in 1948 I found Prof. Alsdorf and his family in a small village in the Eifel, a hilly area of the Rhineland, where he was quietly working on the reconstruction of the late Prof. Lüders' monumental work on Varuṇa; parts of the manuscript had been rescued from a saltmine where Lüders' unpublished materials had been stored for safety. I rejoined Prof. Alsdorf's Seminar at

Münster University and later followed him to Hamburg where he succeeded his Guru Prof. Walther Schubring.

Prof. Alsdorf was keen to give his students an allround Indological education ranging from Vedic and Classical Sanskrit to Jaina Prakrit, Pāli, Old Hindī and modern Indian languages of which he knew Hindī and Urdū well. His personal kindness and ever ready scholarly advice helped me and my fellow-students to overcome the many problems which a non-Indian student of Sanskrit and Middle-Indian is faced with. Textual studies combined with exact philological work of analysis and interpretation were supplemented by his unforgettable lectures on specific historical periods, on art like the Stūpas of India and, last not least, a brilliant one on the monuments of Delhi. The latter Seminar has always remained vividly in my mind, and so familiar was I with this city that I felt like coming home when I finally arrived in Delhi in 1953.

Breaking away from the Seminar in Hamburg ended a chapter in my life but not my close relations with my Guru who never minded that I had not chosen a university career but joined the Foreign Service. We continued meeting in Delhi as Prof. Alsdorf did not belong to those Indologists who bury themselves in their texts and forget about the living reality of India. He must have been the most travelled among our Sanskrit scholars. Every opportunity to come to India was utilised by him to renew his contacts with Indian scholars some of whom he had first met in 1930-32 and to participate as the leading and quite often the only German delegate in Oriental and particularly in Jaina conferences. It was in Ujjain in 1972—and I had the pleasure of accompanying him to this Congress—that after his learned lecture in the Section for Jaina Studies, Prof. Alsdorf was asked by Dr. Dandekar to take part in a special discussion concerning the dates of the Mahabharata War. Not being an expert in the subject, he felt quite embarrassed to speak on such a highly controversial matter. But he dealt with it brilliantly from a Western Indologist's point of view and without hurting the religious feelings of his Indian counterparts.

In his later years Prof. Alsdorf extended his study tours to what he rightfully called "Greater India". He was interested in tracing the spread of Indian culture in Cambodia, Indonesia and Bali. I was fortunate enough to be invited in 1969 to join a family excursion to these countries and to experience Angkor, the great Borobodur and the temples and dances of Bali under his guidance. His tremendous zest for adventure pervaded us all when, in the break of dawn, we headed on ponies for Mount Bromo, an active vulcano in Eastern Java where remnants of a Hindu population were supposed to practice vulcano worship.

On his last visit to India in October-November 1974, Prof. Alsdorf was greatly honoured by the Jaina Community of Delhi. I have witnessed how touched he was when a scroll was presented to him in a silver casket awarding him, on behalf of the Jaina Vishvabharati (Ladnun/Rajasthan), the title 'Jaina-Vijjā-Maṇīshi'. It had been his ardent wish to go with his wife on a *yātra* to the holy places of the Jainas in Rajasthan, Gujarat and Saurashtra. This tour of Ranakpur, Dilwara, Kumbhariya, Shatrunjaya and Girnar was to him a genuine pilgrimage to living Jainism which he understood as a strong force in Indian spirituality past and present.

In the last month of his life Prof. Alsdorf again travelled East to Sri Lanka, a country which was specially dear to him. On a happy postcard from Hikkaduwa he—as so often before—invited me to join him and his wife on their next visit to the island in March 1979. This is now not to be. Prof. Alsdorf died on the 25th of last month in Buchholz near Hamburg as a consequence of an infection which he contracted while visiting the Buddhist sites in Sri Lanka.

> puṣpāṇīva vicinvantam anyatra gatamānasam/
> anavāpteṣu kāmeṣu mṛtyur abhyeti mānavam//

> Death comes to man before he has achieved his wishes
> While he, as if plucking flowers, thinks of something else.

Prof. Jitendra Jetly, Munimaharaj Punyavijayaji, and Prof. Ludwig Alsdorf in the Dharamshala of Jaisalmer (1951)

PROF. K. BRUHN (BERLIN)

OBITUARY

LUDWIG ALSDORF (1904-1978)*

ON THE 25TH OF MARCH, 1978, in the District Hospital at Buchholz near Hamburg, Ludwig Alsdorf died at the age of seventythree. Closely associated with the scholarly tradition of Hermann Jacobi, Heinrich Lüders, Ernst Leumann and Walther Schubring, he served the cause of Indology for half a century. For twentytwo years he was a professor at the University of Hamburg, and he played a decisive part in the subsequent expansion of the Seminar für Kultur und Geschichte Indiens (Department for Indian History and Culture) of that university. He possessed an excellent knowledge of modern India and promoted in Germany—both within and beyond the confines of the academic world — a better understanding of India.

Ludwig Alsdorf was born on the 8th of August, 1904, in Laufersweiler (near Kirchberg in the Hunsrück), the son of the vicar Hermann Alsdorf and Emilie Alsdorf (née Chelius). The family lived in Laufersweiler until 1911, when they moved to Scheidt near Saarbrücken. Alsdorf's father won himself a name as an amateur astronomer, and at the turn of the century he published a number of articles on "selenography" (the geography of the moon) and other astronomical subjects. Through her mother (whose maiden name was Bruch), Alsdorf's mother was related to the famous German composer Max Bruch (1838–1920).[1] Versatility and breadth of interest ran in the family, and they helped to form Alsdorf's character, as did also the atmosphere of the German rectory and the rural background in which he grew up. Having received his schooling at the Ludwigs-Gymnasium at Saarbrücken, he enrolled in 1922 at the University of

*Translated into English by Arthur Tomson († 1981)

1. Emilie Chelius was a granddaughter of Christian Jacob Bruch, paternal uncle of Max Bruch.

Heidelberg, where for two semesters he studied Comparative Philology with Christian Bartholomae and Indology with Heinrich Zimmer. In 1923 he left Heidelberg and went to Hamburg, where he continued his study of Indology with Walther Schubring, graduating in 1928 with a thesis in the field of Jainism that had been suggested to him by Schubring. In the winter of 1929, following Schubring's advice, Alsdorf moved to Berlin to study with Heinrich Lüders. In the following year, through the mediation of Lüders, he was given an opportunity of going for a year and a half (from October 1930 to May 1932) as Reader in German and French to the University of Allahabad, the Vice-Chancellor of which at the time was Ganganath Jha. Alsdorf made use of his stay in India in a number of ways. He photographed manuscripts which he needed for his habilitation thesis on which he had already started to work, acquired a deeper knowledge of Sanskrit with a pandit; and travelled extensively in India, Burma and Ceylon. He returned to Germany in 1932, and in 1934 he completed his habilitation thesis in Berlin. The subject of this thesis, which was again taken from the field of Jaina studies, had been proposed to him by Jacobi in 1928. The habilitation took place in 1935 at the Friedrich-Wilhelms-Universität in Berlin - just in time to be held with the participation of Lüders, who shortly before had been obliged to resign against his will. Alsdorf regularly attended the meetings of the "Kränzchen" ("little garland", hence "private circle") which Lüders held as a substitute for his former official teaching activity. After some years as a university lecturer, in 1938 Alsdorf yielded to the political pressure that had been brought to bear on him in Berlin and transferred his academic activities to Münster (Westfalen). In 1940 his volume *Indien* was published in the series "Weltpolitische Bücherei" (World Political Publications). On the strength of this book, and after a short period of military service with the German occupation forces in France, he was posted in 1941 to the Foreign Office, where until the end of the war he was on the staff of the "Sonderreferat Indien" (Special Section for Indian Affairs) which was set up after the arrival of Subhas Chandra Bose in Germany. Back in Berlin, he was at the same time called upon to teach at the "Auslandswissenschaftliche Fakultät" (Faculty for Studies of Foreign Countries) of the University. In 1944 he was invited to take up a newly founded readership in "Volks- und Landeskunde Indiens" (India: Economics, Politics and Society) at the same Faculty. As the "Auslandswissenschaftliche Fakultät" was not reestablished after the war, Alsdorf at first found himself without a situation and also without a home, for he had been bombed out. Together with his family, he therefore spent the difficult early post-war years with relatives in the countryside at Oberdreis in the Westerwald. In 1948 he was able to return to his old university, Münster, as a 'visiting professor', and in 1950 he was appointed to what was then the only professorship at the Department for Indian History and Culture (now Institute for the Culture and History of India and Tibet) of the University of Hamburg. Here he was the third occupant of the chair of Indology, the first two having been Sten Konow (1914-1920) and Walther Schubring (1920-1950). He took up his residence in Sprötze, a village near Buchholz (to the south of Hamburg). From 1953 to 1954 Alsdorf was Dean of the former Faculty of Humanities of the University of Hamburg. In 1961 he declined an invitation to accept the professorship of Indian Philology at the South-Asia Institute of the University of Heidelberg. — In 1950 Alsdorf was elected a member of the Mainzer Akademie der Wissenschaften und Literatur (Mainz Academy of Sciences and Literature), in 1958 a member of the Joachim Jungius-Gesellschaft der Wissenschaften (Joachim Jungius-Society for Arts and Sciences) in Hamburg, in 1959 a member of the German UNESCO Commission, in 1967 a member of the Kgl. Danske Videnskabernes Selskab (Royal Danish Academy of Sciences), in 1968 Editor-in-Chief of the *Critical Pāli Dictionary* (CPD) and in 1977 a corresponding member of the Österreichische Akademie der Wissenschaften (Austrian Academy of Sciences). In 1977 the Asiatic Society awarded him the S.C. Chakravarty Medal for his work in the field of Indian languages. — In 1972 Alsdorf retired from official duties, but continued to teach until the winter semester of 1977/1978. While on a journey to Ceylon in March 1978 he was stung by an insect. This was at first thought to be harmless, and even after his return to Germany the dangerous consequences were not immediately recognized. However, complications soon set in which led to an embolism of the lung and a few days later caused his death. The sudden turn for the worse spared Alsdorf what might have been a long period of suffering. For his family, his friends and his colleagues at home and abroad, his completely unexpected death came as all the more of a shock.

Alsdorf's many-sidedness makes it difficult to give a concise appreciation of his achievements in research. As a list of his publications down to the year 1974 is already available (cf. p. 15-32), we shall here merely set out the main facts.

The years before the Second World War represent the first phase in Alsdorf's research work. The thesis he wrote at the age of twentythree bears the title *Der Kumārapālapratibodha.* Its subtitle—Studies in Apabhraṃśa and in the Narrative Literature of the Jainas (Engl. Translation)—can be taken as the heading over almost all the publications of the period from 1928 to 1939. Then came the habilitation thesis *Harivaṃśapurāṇa* being a study in the relevant section of Puṣpadanta's Apabhraṃśa version of the World-History of the Jainas. An additional factor here was the discovery that Saṅghadāsa's *Vasudevahiṇḍi* (which belongs to the Harivaṃśa section of the Jaina mythology) is nothing less than "a new version of the lost Bṛhatkathā of Guṇādhya". It may be mentioned in passing that both these works follow the scheme adopted by Jacobi in his earlier publications on Apabhraṃśa works (*Bhavisatta Kaha* and *Sanatkumāracaritam*, 1918 and 1921). An essay on Richard Pischel's *Materialien zur Kenntnis des Apabhraṃśa* (Sources for the Study of Apabhraṃśa, published in 1933) is illuminating in that it shows what sureness of touch Alsdorf had at his command even at that time when dealing with philological matters. The more extensive *Apabhraṃśa-Studien* followed in 1937.

During the war years Alsdorf had to put aside research work in the proper sense of the word. Nevertheless his volume *Indien* (History of the British Rule and the Indian Freedom Movement) appeared in 1940. 1942 saw the publication of his book on *Deutsch-Indische Geistesbeziehungen* (India and Germany: Two Civilizations Meet), which, being the only general survey of its kind, is still consulted today. *Indien und Ceylon* (a concise geography) came out in 1943.

After 1945 his activities suffered from a lack of organic continuity. A number of circumstances obliged Alsdorf to occupy himself with the most varied tasks which— although undertaken voluntarily—noticeably encroached upon his freedom of choice in matters of research. Work on *Varuṇa* and the *Critical Pāli*

Dictionary consumed his time, and the "Landes- und Kulturkunde" *Vorderindien* (India, The Land and the People) was not the sort of book that could be written in a hurry. And while old projects such as the *Vasudevahiṇḍi* were still waiting to be attended to, his teaching duties and other inducements were always opening up new opportunities for research which he did not wish to leave untouched.

Varuṇa, which had to be edited from Lüders' posthumous papers, required Alsdorf's attention until 1959, the year in which the second volume was published. The "Preliminary Remarks" of the editor (pp. III-V) and the considerably longer General "Preface" pp. VII-XII) deserve careful reading because, quite apart from other considerations, they are among the very few comments from Alsdorf's pen that contain an autobiographical element. Lüders, so we are told, had wished to see the two volumes of *Varuṇa* published together. Although Vol. 1 was ready for the press during his lifetime, he did not like the idea of having it issued separately, and he had requested Alsdorf to arrange for its publication in the event of his dying before being able to attend to this himself. This is in fact what happened. Lüders died in 1943, and due to the circumstances then prevailing the manuscript was first deposited in the steel safe of the Berlin Academy of Sciences, whence it was subsequently removed (in accordance with the usual measures taken at the time to protect cultural treasures from the bombing raids) to a salt-mine in Wintershall, which meant that at least initially it was in a safe place. All this happened "without a photocopy having been made, although the need for one had repeatedly been stressed at the meeting of the Kränzchen". In July of 1945 the salt-mine was robbed. The boxes containing Lüders' papers "were stolen because of their usefulness as a means of transport, while their contents, which were of no interest to the robbers, were scattered". Nevertheless a disordered and no longer complete bundle of papers finally arrived in Göttingen in January 1947. The necessary steps were discussed by Waldschmidt and Alsdorf. Details of this cooperation have been described by Waldschmidt[2]. Eventually, the material was transferred to Oberdreis, Alsdorf's aforementioned retreat after the war. In the "Preface" Alsdorf mentions,

2. Zeitschrift der Deutschen Morgenländischen Gesellschaft 130, 180, pp. 34-35.

among many other things, "the beginnings of text formulations, sketches and drafts, all written by preference on waste-paper of every imaginable origin (and thereby sometimes datable)". In the manner of a skilful restorer Alsdorf had to put the whole together again—and also to fit together what had never been a whole. After the work had been done he conceded at the end of the General Preface the following: "We have in front of us (in 1959 Ed.), expositions written twenty, thirty or more years ago which the reader of today will in some cases find out of date". A break-through in the field concerned, or at any rate an important aid to research? It is the specialists who will have the last word. It is, however, incontrovertible that no student of the Vedas can afford to ignore the eight hundred or so pages that make up the two volumes.

At the 24th International Congress of Orientalists held in Munich in 1957, at Alsdorf's instigation the following resolution was passed within the framework of the section for Indology: "that the said Academy (the Royal Danish Academy) with the assistance of the Royal Danish Government will take the necessary steps for a resumption of the work on the *Critical Pāli Dictionary* and ensure its speedy completion". This project, which had been launched under the auspices of the Royal Academy, was brought to a halt after the publication of the first volume (Vol. I, 1924-48, letter ă) by the death of the two editors, H. Smith (Lund) and D. Andersen (Copenhagen). To go into the details of the subsequent vicissitudes of the CPD would be out of place here. Projects of this magnitude are necessarily dependent on institutional planning, and in the case of Indology such planning can be assured (if at all) only in India itself. After 1957, Alsdorf was entrusted with the exacting task of acting as co-ordinator and collaborator, and he carried out these duties in varying official capacities (finally as Editor-in-Chief) until shortly before his death. Fascicles II 1-9 (down to *upakkama*) were issued during his lifetime, II 10 (the proofs of which he had read himself) came out after his death, and II 11-15 followed later. Work on the CPD is being continued under the Editorship of K.R. Norman. Alsdorf once put the matter as follows: "the project still has a very long journey in front of it". He soon recognized the difficulties which unavoidably arose in spite of an intensive collaboration between Pāli specialists in different countries, and he knew more clearly than on any previous occasions that his powers had here come up against a limit.

When one considers the history of earlier German Indology, Alsdorf's "Landes- und Kulturkunde" *Vorderindien* published in 1955 by the Georg Westermann Verlag and covering the entire subcontinent, was a notable achievement. It was a modern book, and it was written with great industry and prudence by a man whose chief preoccupations lay in another domain. How well the book was received is shown by the fact that the publisher later approached Alsdorf with the request that he should prepare a revised version. But Alsdorf had to decline for a number of reasons, not the least of which was that in the intervening years history had not stood still. A "Landes- und Kulturkunde" is perhaps more urgently needed now than in those days, but in view of the increase in knowledge projects of this kind will no longer come up to academic standards unless they are limited in scope to a selected region.

The *Vasudevahiṇḍi* was a discovery in two respects. On the one hand it was found to be a new version of the lost *Bṛhatkathā*, and on the other hand it was the oldest compact narrative work of the Jainas to have survived, to say nothing of its archaic language and metre. As things stood in the nineteen-thirties, when Alsdorf's colleagues heard of the discovery, they were bound to assume that a full treatment of the *Vasudevahiṇḍi* would become his life's work. The discoverer did not conceal his find. He published a number of studies devoted to the text, perhaps he also said almost all that could be said of basic importance after a first working through of the text. But he never got around to preparing an exhaustive publication. Although the first communication on the subject, written in English, had already appeared in the *Bulletin of the School of Oriental Studies*, Vol. 8 (1935/1937), international Indology only gradually took notice of the matter.

Since Alsdorf never gave up the idea of working on the *Vasudevahiṇḍi*, it seemed pertinent to mention the matter in connection with Alsdorf's studies after the war. But after the war he rarely found an opportunity of taking the work up again. Such time as was left to him after attending to his duties in connection with the aforementioned projects—that is, such time as was available to him for research on his own choice - he would spend on other interests. The inscriptions of Aśoka (to which Lüders had introduced him in Berlin), the Jātakas (another subject which had played a major part in Lüders' own research), and the metrical *Uttarādhyayanasūtra* of the Jaina canon were the texts to which Alsdorf paid special attention. In addition there were topics such as vegetarianism and Pāli prosody for which he had to consult more than one text. It is not easy to classify or to assess these studies from a few points of view, and the fact that this cannot be done is indeed characteristic of the period in question. But in view of the special position of Jainist studies, it seems appropriate here to point out that soon after the war Alsdorf recommenced his work in the field of Jaina literature and, in addition to the *Uttarādhyayana* studies mentioned above, continued it on more than one level. During the last years of his life he came closer and closer, and quite intentionally so, to Leumann's Jainological studies (mainly *Āvaśyakaniryukti* and Jinabhadra's *Viśeṣāvaśyakabhāṣya*). In an article which, although written earlier. was not published until 1977, he refers to the need "to resume Leumann's work and to continue it". Let us add that an appreciation of Alsdorf's many-sided contacts with India and with Indian colleagues can only be enhanced by a reference to the particularly close connections he established on his numerous visits to India with Jaina scholars, monks and laymen.

Alsdorf repeatedly described his second teacher Lüders as a master of the philological method: "Lüders possessed in a very high degree what he himself liked to call the most essential requirement of a philologist: a feeling for the probable. This was put into practice in connection with a method that knew no compromise and in its rigour tolerated no easy way out". This statement should not, however, in any way be taken to imply that Alsdorf did not go his own way. He liked to show that sizeable texts and layers of texts, on which a fair amount of research had already been done, suddenly took on a new appearance when subjected to penetrating analysis. He also liked, in passing, to draw attention to subjects that had been by-passed by other scholars. He discovered so many things that he could never have afforded to devote a detailed study *to every find* or to give a systematic elucidation on every observation involving *method*.

Alsdorf's approach to the texts he studied can be called "straight". What mattered to him was not so much the amassing of material but rather a sharpness of judgement which, often removing errors perpetuated by centuries of textual transmission, enabled him to restore the correct reading. In this he was guided above all by a feeling for language, a training in Indian linguistics and an acute ear for metre. Furthermore, he showed a rare awareness of the differences in mentality of the authors of Jātaka verse and Jātaka prose, and he was one of the first to demonstrate, on the basis of a selected example, the conceptual acrobatics of the Jaina dogmatists. This broad receptivity, allied as it was to a critical and academically fruitful sympathy for India both ancient and modern, enabled him to see more than others.

A scholar's achievements are not confined to his published works alone. In the case of Ludwig Alsdorf it would certainly be unjust not to mention his qualities as a teacher. When lecturing he would captivate his colleagues and his students, both Indologists and non-specialists. A larger academic discipline would have given his talents greater scope. A larger number of students would have assured him a wider, and a more timely, appreciation of his scientific work. It is, however, pointless to speculate now on what might have been granted him in the way of a more ample recognition. Alsdorf did what lay in his power and what circumstances enabled him to do. His work is now in the hands of others, and others will have to complete what he left unfinished.

PROF. A. WEZLER (HAMBURG)

BIBLIOGRAPHY OF THE WRITINGS OF LUDWIG ALSDORF*

I. Books and monographs.—II. Essays: 1. Articles, lectures and reports: A. Veda — B. Jainism. — C. Buddhism. — D. Aśokan and other inscriptions.—E. Middle Indo-Aryan. — F. Literature, culture and art. — G. History. — H. Indigenous sciences. — I. New Indo-Aryan. — J. Modern India. — K. History of Indology. — L. Travelogues. — M. Miscellanea. 2. Reviews and notices. 3. Obituaries. — III. Editorial activity. — IV. Articles on Ludwig Alsdorf. — V. Addenda.

Abbreviations

Akad. d. Wiss. u.d. Lit. Abh. Geistes- u. Sozialwissenschaftliche Kl. = Akademie der Wissenschaften und der Literatur, Abhandlungen. Geistes- und Sozialwissenschaftliche Klasse
AKM = Abhandlungen für die Kunde des Morgenlandes
ALB = Adyar Library Bulletin
Alt- u. Neu-Indische Studien = Alt- und Neu-Indische Studien, herausgegeben vom Seminar für Kultur und Geschichte Indiens an der Hamburgischen Universität
BDCRI = Bulletin of the Deccan College Research Institute
BSOAS = Bulletin of the School of Oriental and African Studies
DLZ = Deutsche Literaturzeitung
EI = Epigraphia Indica
GeoR = Geographische Rundschau
HZ = Historische Zeitschrift
IIJ = Indo-Iranian Journal
IL = Indian Linguistics
JOAS = Journal of the American Oriental Society
JOI = Journal of the Oriental Institute (Baroda)

*Updated reprint from : L. Alsdorf, Kleine Schriften ed. by A. Wezler Glasenapp—Stiftung Vol. 10. Franz Steiner Verlag GmbH, Wiesbaden 1974.

NIA = New Indian Antiquary
OLZ = Orientalistische Literaturzeitung
WZKSO = Wiener Zeitschrift für die Kunde Sud- und Ostasiens; seit Bd. 14 (1970) WZKS = Wiener Zeitschrift für die Kunde Südasiens
ZDMG = Zeitschrift der Deutschen Morgenländischen Gesellschaft.
ZfGeop = Zeitschrift für Geopolitik
ZfP = Zeitschrift für Politik
ZII = Zeitschrift für Indologie und Iranistik

I. BOOKS AND MONOGRAPHS

1. Der Kumārapālapratibodha. Ein Beitrag zur Kenntnis des Apabhraṃśa und der Erzählungsliteratur der Jainas. Von Ludwig Alsdorf. Hamburg: Friederichsen, de Gruyter & Co. 1928. XII, 227 S. 4°. (Dissertation). (Alt- u. Neu-Indische Studien. 2.).
2. Harivaṃśapurāṇa. Ein Abschnitt aus der Apabhraṃśa-Welthistorie "Mahāpurāṇa Tisaṭṭhimahāpurisaguṇālaṃkāra" von Puṣpadanta. Als Beitrag zur Kenntnis des Apabhraṃśa und der Universalgeschichte der Jainas hrsg. von Ludwig Alsdorf. Mit. 3 Taf. Hamburg: Friederiehsen, de Gruyter & Co. 1936. XII, 515 S. 4°, Zugleich Berlin, Phil. Hab.-Schrift. (Alt- u. Neu-Indische Studien. 5.).
3. Apabhraṃśa-Studien. Von Ludwig Alsdorf. Leipzig: Brockhaus in Komm. 1937. VIII, 113 S. 8°. (AKM XXII, 2.). [Nachdruck: Nendeln, Liechtenstein: Kraus 1966.]
4. Indien. Berlin: Deutscher Verlag 1940. 242 S. mit 8 Karten. 8°. Zweite durchgesehene Auflage 1941, 4. Auflage 1943. (Weltpolitische Bücherei. Herausgegeben von Georg Leibbrandt und Egmont Zechlin.)
5. India Inglesa. Por Ludwig Alsdorf. Tradución directa del alemán. Por Luis de Navia. Madrid: Ediciones España 1942. 238 S. 8°.
6. Deutsch-Indische Geistesbeziehungen. Von Ludwig Alsdorf. Mit 4 Abb. Heidelberg, Berlin, Magdeburg: Vowinckel 1942. VII, 111 S. 8°. (2. Aufl.?) 1944. (Indien in Einzeldarstellungen. Herausgegeben von Kurt Vowinckel. Bd. 7).
7. Indien und Ceylon. Berlin: Junker und Dünnhaupt 1943. 159 S., mehrere Karten. 8°. (Kleine Auslandskunde. Herausgegeben von Prof. Dr. F. A. Six. Bd. 29/30.).

8. Pantschatantra. Fünf Bücher altindischer Staatsweisheit und Lebenskunst in Fabeln und Sprüchen. Hrsg. u. übers. von Ludwig Alsdorf. Bergen II, Oberbayern: Müller & Kiepenheuer 1952. 124 S. 8°. (Die Weltliteratur. Nr 96/99.).
9. Vorderindien. Bharat, Pakistan, Ceylon. Eine Landes- und Kulturkunde. Mit 23 Karten und Diagrammen und 59 Abb. Braun-schweig, Berlin, Hamburg [usw.]: Westermann 1955. 336 S. 8°.
10. Beiträge zur Geschichte von Vegetarismus und Rinderverehrung in Indien. Von Ludwig Alsdorf. Mainz: Akad.; Wiesbaden: Steiner in Komm. 1962. 69 S. 8°. (Akad. d. Wiss. u. d. Lit. Abh. Geistes- u. Sozialwissenschaftliche Kl. Jg. 1961, Nr. 6. S. 557–625).
11. Aśokas Separatedikte von Dhauli und Jaugaḍa. Von Ludwig Alsdorf. Mainz: Akad.; Wiesbaden: Steiner in Komm. 1962. 38 S. 8°. (Akad. d. Wiss. u. d. Lit. Abh. Geistes- und Sozialwissenschaftliche Kl. Jg. 1962, Nr. 1. S. 1-38).... 464
12. The Āryā Stanzas of the Uttarajhāyā. Contributions to the Text History and Interpretation of a Canonical Jaina Text. By Ludwig Alsdorf. Mainz: Akad.; Wiesbaden: Steiner in Komm. 1966. 68 S. 8°. (Akad. d. Wiss. u. d. Lit. Abh. Geistes - und Sozialwissenschaftliche Kl.J g. 1966, Nr. 2. S. 153–220).
13. Les Études Jaina, État présent et tâches futures. Conférences par Ludwig Alsdorf. [Paris]: Collège de France 1965 (1966). 97 S. 8°.
14. Die Āryā-Strophen des Pali-Kanons. Metrisch hergestellt und textgeschichtlich untersucht. Von Ludwig Alsdorf. Mainz: Akad.; Wiesbaden: Steiner in Komm. 1968. 89 S. 8°. (Akad. d. Wiss. u. d. Lit. Abh. Geistes und Sozialwissenschaftliche Kl. Jg. 1967, Nr. 4. S. 243-331).

II. ESSAYS

1. ARTICLES, LECTURES AND REPORTS

A. VEDA

15. Contributions to the Textual Criticism of the Kaṭhopaniṣad. ZDMG 100. 1950 (erschienen 1951), S. 621-637.... 1
16. Gleanings from the Atharvaveda. ALB 25. 1961, S.106-116 18

B. Jainism

30. Itthīparinnā. A Chapter of Jain Monastic Poetry, edited as a Contribution to Indian Prosody. IIJ 2. 1958. S. 249-270. 193
31. Namipavvajjā: Contributions to the Study of a Jain Canonical Legend. In: Indological Studies in Honor of W. Norman Brown. Ed. by E. Bender. New Haven 1962, S. 8-17. 215
32. Uttarajjhāyā Studies. IIJ 6. 1962, S. 110-136.......... 225
33. What were the Contents of the Dṛṣṭivāda? In: German Scholars on India. Contributions to Indian Studies edited by the Cultural Department of the Embassy of the Federal Republic of Germany, New Delhi. Vol. I. Benares 1973, S. 1-5 252
34. Nikṣepa—A Jaina Contribution to Scholastic Methodology. JOI 22. 1973, S. 455-463 257

C. BUDDHISM

35. Bemerkungen zu einem metrischen Fragment des Mahāparinirvāṇasūtra. ZDMG 105. 1955, S. 327-330. ... 266
36. Bemerkungen zum Vessantara-Jātaka. WZKSO 1. 1957, S. 1-70. 270
37. *Sahadhammiko vādânuvādo gārayhaṃ ṭhānaṃ āgacchati.* ZDMG 109. 1959, S. 317-323........................ 340
38. Śaśa-Jātaka und Śaśa-Avadāna. WZKSO 5. 1961, S. 1-17. 347
39. Āryā Stanzas in the Thera—Therī-Gâthā. Appendix II in: The Thera- and Therī-Gâthâ: (Stanzas ascribed to Elders of the Buddhist Order of Recluses) ed. by H. Oldenberg and R. Pischel. Second edition with Appendices by K.R. Norman and L. Alsdorf. London 1966, S. 233-250.
40. Das Sivijātaka (499): Ein Beitrag zu seiner Textgeschichte. In: Pratidānam. Indian, Iranian and Indo-European Studies presented to Franciscus Bernardus Jacobus Kuiper on his sixtieth Birthday. Ed. by J.C. Heesterman, G.H. Schokker, V.J. Subramoniam. Den Haag 1968, S. 478-483 364
41. Verkannte Mahāvastu-Strophen. In: Beiträge zur Geistesgeschichte Indiens. Festschrift für Erich Frauwallner. Aus Anlaß seines 70. Geburtstages herausgegeben von G. Ober-

D. Aśokan and other inscriptions

E. Middle Indo-Aryan

F. Literature, Culture and Art

G. History

55. Indien von der mohammedanischen Eroberung bis zur Gegenwart. In: Geschichte Asiens von E. Waldschmidt, L. Alsdorf, B. Spuler, H.O.H. Stange und O. Kressler. (Weltgeschichte in Einzeldarstellungen.). München: F. Bruckmann 1950, S. 163-307.
56. Indien und das neuzeitliche Abendland. In: Europäisch-Asiatischer Dialog. Vorträge der Tagung in Bottrop vom 25. bis 28. Oktober 1955. Hrsg. vom Vorstand des Landesverbandes nordrhein-westfälischer Geschichtslehrer. Düsseldorf 1956. S. 32-46.
57. Vorderindien und Ceylon. In: Bücherkunde zur Weltgeschichte vom Untergang des Römischen Reiches bis zur Gegenwart, bearbeitet von Günther Franz. München 1956, S. 380-388 (Nr. 5471-5601).
58. Indien. Sonderausgabe aus dem Jahrbuch der Weltpolitik 1943. Deutsches Auslandswissenschaftliches Institut. Berlin 1943, S. 637-658.

H. Indigenous Sciences

I. New Indo-Aryan

61. The Origin of the New Indo-Aryan Speeches. Translated from Original German by S. N. Ghosal, Calcutta. JOI 10. 1960-61, S. 129-146.
62. Die indischen Sprachen und das Englische in Indien. "Parlament". Die Woche im Bundestag. Nr. 33-34/16. 8. 1961. S. 16

J. MODERN INDIA

63. Die indische Freiheitsbewegung. ZDMG 96. 1942, S. *49*-*52* (Bericht über die Arbeitstagung der deutschen Orientalisten).
64. Britisch-Indien in der Weltpolitik und Weltwirtschaft. Vortrag in der Deutschen Weltwirtschaftlichen Gesellschaft in Berlin am 27. Febr. 1942. Weltwirtschaft 30. 1942, S. 67-73.
65. Die indische Freiheitsbewegung. In: Der Orient in deutscher Forschung. Vorträge der Berliner Orientalistentagung Herbst 1942. Hrsg. von Hans Heinrich Schaeder (=Deutsche Orientforschung). Leipzig 1944, S. 217-227.
66. Das Flüchtlingsproblem in Indien. [1.] Sonderheft der Zeitschrift für Raumforschung 1950, S. 111-115.
67. Mahatma Gandhi, der Repräsentant und Erneuerer indischen Geistes. Missionswissenschaft und Religionswissenschaft 35. 1951, S. 45-68.......................... 686
68. Wirtschaftsprobleme des Neuen Indien. GeoR 4. 1952, S. 241-249.
69. Das Flüchtlingsproblem in Indien. Der Hafen. Monatsschrift des Hamburger Hafen-Vereins von 1872. Sonderheft—India—Special Issue. Hamburg 1955, S. 22-23. [Engl. Übersetzung "The Indian Refugee Problem", S. 24].
70. Rassen und Sprachen in Indien. GeoR 7. 1955, S. 373-382.
71. Indien in Zahlen. GeoR 7. 1955, S. 405-409. Bildbeilage "Bilder aus Indien" (Abb. 1-8) nebst Erläuterungen "Zu den Bildern aus Indien", S. 410-411.
72. Das indische Kastenwesen. GeoR 8. 1956, S. 215-219.
73. Indien im Umbruch. Vortrag von L. Alsdorf. Hamburgisches Welt-Wirtschafts-Archiv 1956. (Protokoll: Erstes Mittwochsgespräch des Hamburgischen Welt-Wirtschafts-Archivs im Übersee-Club am 31. Oktober 1956), S. 1-6.

74. Indien und sein Verhältnis zu den Machtblöcken. In: Das Ende der Kolonialzeit und die Welt von morgen. Eine Vortragsreihe. Mit Beiträgen von L. Alsdorf [u.a.]. Buchausgabe der gleichnamigen Sendereihe des Süddeutschen Rundfunks. (Kröners Taschenausgabe. Bd. 338.). (Das Heidelberger Studio. Sendefolge 23). Stuttgart 1961, S. 63-75 710
75. Das heutige Indien im Spiegel seiner Geschichte. Geschichte in Wissenschaft und Unterricht. Zeitschrift des Verbandes der Geschichtslehrer Deutschlands. 12. 1961. S. 283-297.

K. HISTORY OF INDOLOGY

76. Max Müller. India Magazine. A German Review for India 2. 1955, S. 39-40.
77. Die Indologie in Berlin von 1821-1945. In: Studium Berolinense. Aufsätze und Beiträge zu Problemen der Wissenschaft und der Geschichte der Friedrich-Wilhelms-Universität zu Berlin. Hrsg. von H. Leussink, E. Neumann und G. Kotowski. (Gedenkschrift der Westdeutschen Rektorenkonferenz und der Freien Universität Berlin zur 150. Wiederkehr des Gründungsjahres der Friedrich-Wilhelms-Universität zu Berlin. 2.) Berlin 1960, S. 567-580 723
78. Der Stand der Indologie in Deutschland. Moderne Welt. Zeitschrift für vergleichende geistesgeschichtliche und sozialwissenschaftliche Forschung 2. 1960/61, S. 107-112.
79. Indian Studies in Germany. The Indo-Asian Culture 10, 1962, S. 296-314 und 456-461.
80. New Trends in Indology. Cultural Forum 24 (Ministry of Education. Government of India. Editor: D. K. Hingorani) 6, 1964, S. 54-56.

L. TRAVELOGUES

81. Jaisalmer, die Rajputenburg in der Wüste. GeoR 4. 1952, S. 269-271. Bildbeilage (Abb. 1-7).
82. Fahrt zu Indiens Höhlenklöstern. Westermanns Monatshefte 95. 1954, S. 31-35, mit 5 Abb.

83. Radschputana—Land der Ritter. Westermanns Monatshefte 96. 1955, S. 23-28, mit 5 Abb.
84. Reise nach Nepal. Westermanns Monatshefte 97. 1956, S. 41-47, mit 7 Abb.
85. Bilder aus Nepal. Bildbeilage (Abb. 1-8). GeoR 9. 1957, nebst Erläuterungen "Zu den Bildern aus Nepal", S. 157-159.
86. Nepal. Westermann Dia. Beiheft. Erdkunde. Braunschweig 1959, S. 1-5.

M. Miscellanea

87. In: Meyer's Lexikon. In völlig neuer Bearb. u. Bebilderung. Mit etwa 20000 teils farbigen Abb. im Text u. auf Beil., etwa 400 Haupt u. Nebenkt., 1 Atlasbd. sowie 1 Reg. -Bd. 8. Aufl. Bd. 6 „Japanholz — Kudlich". Leipzig: Bibliographisches Institut 1939. Stichwort "Indische Kultur", Sp. 147-148 (Allgemeine Kulturentwicklung), Sp. 161-163 (Sprachen), Sp. 165-166 (Theater).
88. In: Der Große Herder. Nachschlagwerk für Wissen und Leben. 5., neubearb. Aufl. von Herders Konversationslexikon. Bd. 4 „Georg bis Italien". Freiburg: Verlag Herder 1954. Stichwort „Hinterindien", Sp. 943; Stichwort „Indien", Sp. 1291-1298 (Allgemeine Geschichte), Sp. 1299-1303 (Philosophie, Kunst); Stichwort „Indische Union", Sp. 1312-1315 (Kultur); Stichwort „Indochina", Sp. 1319 (Geschichte).
89. Indien im deutschen Schul-Geographiebuch. Indien — Deutschland. Empfehlungen der indisch-deutschen Historiker-Konferenz Braunschweig 1954. Sonderdruck aus dem Internationalen Jahrbuch für Geschichtsunterricht 1956. Braunschweig 1956, S. 81-99.
90. In: Kindlers Literaturlexikon. (Werklexikon in 7 Bden auf der Grundlage des „Dizionario delle opere di tutti i tempi e di tutte le letterature", hrsg. von Valentino Bompiani. Wissenschaftl. Vorbereitung Wolfgang von Einsiedel unter Mitarb. zahlr. Fachberater. Chefred.: Gert Woerner, Stellvertreter: Gisela Uellenberg). Bd. 1 —. Zürich: Kindler 1965 —. Bd. 6 "Werke Rb — Tz" (1971). Stichworte "Subhāṣitaratnasaṃdoha", Sp. 2062-63; „Syādvādamanjarī", Sp. 2246-47; „Tattvārthādhigamasūtra", Sp. 2440; "Triṣaṣṭi-

śalākāpuruṣacaritra", Sp. 3048-49. Bd. 7 „Werke U - Z. Essays. Register" (1972). Stichworte Upamitibhavaprapañcā Kathā", Sp. 209-10; „Vasudevahiṇḍi", Sp. 331-32; „Yogaśāstra", Sp. 1291.

2. REVIEWS AND NOTICES

91. Shahidullah, M.: Les Chants Mystiques de Kāṇha et de Saraha. Les Dohā-Ḳoṣa (en apabhraṃśa, avec les versions tibétaines) et les Caryā (en vieux-bengali) avec introduction, vocabulaires et notes édités et traduits. Paris 1928. Textes pour l'étude due Bouddhisme tardif. In: OLZ 32. 1929, Sp. 942-952 737
92. Glasenapp, H. von: Von Buddha zu Gandhi. Indisches Denken im Wandel der Jahrhunderte. Tübingen 1934. In: OLZ 38. 1935, Sp). 640.
93. Jain, Hiralal: Karakaṇḍa Cariu of Muni Kanakāmara. Critically edited with Introduction, Translation, Glossary, Indices, Notes and Appendices. Karanja (Berar, India): Karanja Jaina Publication Society 1934=Ambādās Chaware Digambara Jaina Granthamālā or Karanja Jaina Series, Vol. IV. In: OLZ 38. 1935, Sp. 645-651 743
94. Hilgenberg, L.: Die kosmographische Episode im Mahābhārata und Padmapurāṇa, textgeschichtlich untersucht. Stuttgart 1934. In: OLZ 38. 1935, Sp. 704-705.
95. Shah, Shantilal: The traditional Chronology of the Jainas. An Outline of the political development of India from 543 B.C. to 78 A.D. Stuttgart 1935. In: DLZ 56. 1935, Sp. 2167-2169.
96. Grierson, Sir G.A.: The Test of a Man, being the Purusha-Parîkshâ of Vidyâpati Ṭhakkura, translated into English. London 1935. In: OLZ 39. 1936, Sp. 552-555.
97. Schubring, W.: Die Lehre der Jainas nach den alten Quellen dargestellt. Berlin and Leipzig 1935 (Grundriß der indo-arischen Philologie und Altertumskunde III. Bd., 7. H.). In: DLZ 57. 1936, Sp. 917-921.
98. Kâpaḍiyâ, Hîrâlâl Rasikdâs: Ārhat jivan jyoti (kiraṇavali 1-4). Bombay 1934-36. In: OLZ 40. 1937., Sp. 454-455.
99. Chaudhuri, Nagendra N.: Studies in the Apabhraṃśa Texts

of the Dākārṇava (Text from Nepal, 2). Calcutta 1935. In: OLZ 40. 1937, Sp. 554-557.

100. Sharma, Venkatesh N.: Indische Erziehung. Weimar 1936. Rez. unter der Überschrift "Indische Erziehung" in: Die Erziehung. Monatsschrift für den Zusammenhang von Kultur und Erziehung in Wissenschaft und Leben 12. 1937, S. 284-286.
101. Sen, Amulyachandra: A Critical Introduction to Paṇhāvāgaraṇāiṃ, the tenth Anga of the Jaina Canon. Diss. Hamburg 1936. In: OLZ 41. 1938, Sp. 448-450.
102. Dillon, M.: The Nāṭakalakṣanaratnakośa of Sāgaranandin, ed., Vol. I, Text. London 1937. In: OLZ 41. 1938, Sp. 564-565.
103. Esteller, A.: Die älteste Rezension des „Mahānāṭakam". Ein Beitrag zur Geschichte des indischen Bühnen- und Schattenspiels und der Rāmasage. Leipzig 1937. In: OLZ 41. 1938., Sp. 636-639.
104. Scharpé, A. A. M.: Bāṇa's Kādambarī. Vertaling, van het Sanskrit in het Nederlands, van het Uttarabhāga en van gedeelten van het Pūrvabhāga, met inleiding, aantekeningen en lexicographisch appendix. Leuven 1937. In: DLZ 59. 1938, Sp. 1488-1490.
105. Grierson, Sir G. A.: On the modern Indo-Aryan Vernaculars (an unfinished study). Bombay o. J. In: DLZ 60. 1939, Sp. 368-371.
106. Kohl, J. F.: Die Sūryaprajñapti. Versuch einer Textgeschichte. Stuttgart 1937. In: DLZ 60, 1939, Sp. 729-732.
107. Mackay, E.: Die Induskultur. Ausgrabungen in Mohenjo-Daro und Harappa. Leipzig 1938. In: OLZ 43. 1940, Sp. 122-126.
108. Annual Bibliography of Indian Archaeology. Vol.XII for the year 1937. Leyden 1939. In: OLZ 43. 1940, Sp. 441-443.
109. De, Sushil Kumar: The Kṛṣṇa-Karṇāmṛta of Līlāśuka. A Mediaeval Vaiṣṇava devotional poem in Sanskrit (Bengal Recension). With three Sanskrit Commentaries of the Bengal Vaiṣṇava School, the Kṛṣṇa-Vallabhā of Gopāla Bhaṭṭa, the Subodhanī of Caitanyadāsa and the Śāraṅga-Raṅgadā of Kṛṣṇadāsa Kavirāja. Crtitically edited. With Appendices containing Additional Verses given in the South Indian Version, as well as in the Bilvamaṅgala Kośa-Kāvya, the

Kṛṣṇa-Stotra and other works: Dacca 1938. In: OLZ 43. 1940, Sp. 487-488.

110. Vacca, V.: L'India musulmana. Milano 1941. In: ZfP 32. 1942, S. 361-363.

111. Indien in Einzeldarstellungen. Hrsg. von Kurt Vowinckel. Heidelberg, Berlin, Magdeburg 1941.
   Bd. 1: Dr. Hermann Beythan: Was ist Indien?
   Bd. 2: Dr. Hermann Lufft: Die Wirtschaft Indiens.
   Bd. 4: Mukund Vyas: Männer und Mächte in Indien.
   Bd. 8: Wilhelm Kruse: Denkmäler indischer Kunst.
   In: ZfP 32. 1942, S. 646-649.

112. Dreesen, W.: Indien im Feuer. Bericht einer Reise. Hamburg 1942. — Ahmad, H. Manzooruddin: Indien ohne Wunder. Leipzig 1942. Rez. unter der Überschrift „Indien im Feuer" in: ZfP 33. 1943, S. 421-423.

113. Annual Bibliography of Indian Archaeology. Vol. XIII for the year 1938 and Vol. XIV for the year 1939. Leyden 1940 und 1941. In: OLZ 46. 1943, Sp. 420-423.

114. Spear, P.: Twilight of the Mughuls. Studies in the Late Mughul Delhi. Cambridge 1951. In: HZ 174. 1952, S. 668-669.

115. Wenz, H.: Weltmacht Indien. Nürnberg 1952. Rez. unter der Überschrift „Ein maßgebendes modernes Indienbuch fehlt" in: ZfGeop 23. 1952, S. 246-248.

116. Pörksen, M.: Junge Kirche im freien Indien. Breklum 1951. Rez. unter der Überschrift „Indische Christen" in: ZfGeop 23. 1952, S. 497.

117. Veltheim-Ostrau, H. H. von: Tagebücher aus Asien (Bombay, Kalkutta, Kaschmir, Afghanistan, die Himalayas, Nepal, Benares) 1935-1939. Köln 1951. — Filchner, W.: In der Fieberhölle Nepals. Wiesbaden 1951. — Philips, C. H.: Indien. Berlin 1950. — Steche, H.: Indien — Bharat und Pakistan. Berlin 1952.—Tichy, H.: Die Wandlung des Lotos. Ein Indienbericht. Wien 1951. — Siegfried, A.: Voyage aux Indes. Paris 1951. Rez. unter der Überschrift „Fünf Jahre freies Indien" in: ZfGeop 23. 1952, S. 707-714.

118. David-Neel, A.: Zwischen Göttern und Politik. Indien—gestern, heute, morgen. Wiesbaden 1952. In: Das historisch-politische Buch 1. 1953, S. 32.

119. Schucht, E.: Unter der silbernen Sichel. Eine Reise durch

Pakistan. München 1952. In: Das historisch-politische Buch 1. 1953, S. 64.

120. Nehru, Jawaharlal: Indiens Weg zur Freiheit. Frankfurt 1952. In: Das historisch-politische Buch 1. 1953, S. 125-126.
121. Corbett, J.: Mein Indien. Zürich und Konstanz 1953. In: Das historisch-politische Buch 2. 1954, S. 63.
122. Annual Bibliography of Indian Archaeology. Vol. XV for the years 1940-1947. Leyden 1950. In: OLZ 49. 1954, Sp. 356-358.
123. Gutersohn, H.: Indien. Eine Nation im Werden. Bern 1953. In: Das historisch-politische Buch 2. 1954, S. 95.
124. Filchner W. und Marâthe, Dr. Sridhar: Hindustan im Festgewand. Celle 1953. In: Das historisch-politische Buch 2. 1954, S. 156.
125. Karunakaran, K. P.: India in World Affairs, August 1947 — January 1950. A review of India's foreign relations from Independence Day to Republic Day. Calcutta 1952. Rez. unter der Überschrift „Indische Außenpolitik" in: ZfGeop 25. 1954, S. 628-629.
126. Ancient Jaina Hymns. Critically edited with introduction, discourses, notes and index by Charlotte Krause. Ujjain, Scindia Oriental Institute 1952. Pp. IV-144. (Scindia Oriental Series No. 2). In: Oriens 8. 1955, S. 367-369.
127. Veltheim-Ostrau, H. H. von: Der Atem Indiens. Tagebücher aus Asien. Neue Folge: Ceylon und Südindien. Hamburg 1954. In: Das historisch-politische Buch 3. 1955, S. 220.
128. Ingham, K.: Reformers in India 1793-1833. An account of the work of Christian Missionaries on behalf of social reform. London 1956. In: HZ 184. 1957, S. 712-713.
129. Gode, P. K.: Studies in Indian Literary History. Vol. I, II. Bombay 1953, 1954. Vol. III. Poona 1956. In: ZDMG 107. 1957, S. 214-215.
130. Kirfel, W.: Das Purāṇa vom Weltgebäude (Bhuvanavinyāsa). Die kosmographischen Traktate der Purāṇa's. Versuch einer Textgeschichte. Bonn 1954. In: ZDMG 107. 1957, S. 221-222.
131. Renou, L. et Filliozat, J.: L'Inde classique. Manuel des études indiennes. Tome II. Avec le concours de Paul Demi-

éville, Olivier Lacombe, Pierre Meile. Paris 1953. In: ZDMG 107. 1957, S. 222-225.

132. Basham, A. L.: The wonder that was India. A survey of the culture of the Indian sub-continent before the coming of the Muslims. London 1954. In: ZDMG 107. 1957, S. 225-227.
133. Gedichte des Rig-Veda. Auswahl und Übersetzung von Hermann Lommel. München-Planegg 1955. In: ZDMG 107. 1957, S. 658-660.
134. Deo, Shantaram Bhalchandra: History of Jaina Monachism from Inscriptions and Literature. Poona 1956. In JAOS 78. 1958, S. 319-321.
135. De Golish, V. — Rambach, P. — Stevens, F. Herbert: L'Inde inexplorée. Expédition tortue 1950-1952. Afrique — Moyen-Orient — Indes. Paris 1955. Deutsche Ausgabe (übers. von L. Grambihler): Unerforschtes Indien. Expedition „Schildkröte" 1950-1952. Afrika — Mittlerer Orient — Indien. Biberach/Riss o. J. In: OLZ 53. 1958, Sp. 256-257.
136. Singer, E.: Das Antlitz Indiens. Prag o. J. In: OLZ 53, 1958, Sp. 371-372.
137. Weir, T.: East of Katmandu. London [1955]. In: OLZ 54. 1959, Sp. 195.
138. Annual Bibliography of Indian Archaeology. Vol. XVI for the years 1948-1953. Leyden 1958. In: OLZ 54. 1959, Sp. 519-521.
139. Sen, Surendra Nath: Eighteen Fifty-Seven. With a foreword by Maulana Abul Kalam Azad. Delhi 1957. In: Internationales Jahrbuch für den Geschichtsunterricht 7. 1959/60, S. 389-390.
140. Rech, E.: Il Nepal e la Repubblica popolare cinese. Roma 1957. In: OLZ 55. 1960. Sp. 89.
141. Filliozat, J.: Les relations extérieures de l'Inde (I). Pondichéry 1956. In: OLZ 55. 1960, Sp. 184-186.
142. Hardy, P.: Historians of Medieval India. Studies in Indo-Muslim Historical Writing. London 1960. In: Der Islam. Zeitschrift für Geschichte und Kultur des Islamischen Orients 37. 1961, S. 293-295.
143. Hagen, T. — Wahlen, F.T. — Corti, W. R.: Nepal, Königreich am Himalaya. Bern 1960. In: ZDMG 112. 1962 (erschienen 1963), S. 209-211.

144. Triṣaṣṭiśalākāpuruṣacaritra or The lives of the sixty-three illustrious persons, by Ācārya Śrī Hemacandra. Vol. V. Transl. into English by Helen M. Johnson. Baroda 1962. In: ZDMG 114, 1964, S. 453-455.
145. Gupta, Brijen K.: Sirajudaullah and the East India Company, 1756-1757. Background to the foundation of British power in India. Leiden 1962. In: OLZ 59. 1964, Sp. 393-394.
146. Puṇyavijaya, Āgama Prabhākara Muni: Catalogue of Palm-leaf Manuscripts in the Śāntinātha Jain Bhaṇḍāra, Cambay, I. Baroda 1961. In: OLZ 59. 1964, Sp. 494-495.
147. Annual Bibliography of Indian Archaeology. Vol. XVII for the years 1954-1957. Leyden 1962. In: OLZ 60. 1965, Sp. 184-185.
148. Philips, C. H., with the co-operation of Prof. H. L. Singh and Dr. B. N. Pandey: The Evolution of India and Pakistan 1858-1947. Select Documents. London 1962. In: OLZ 61. 1966, Sp. 81-82.
149. Puṇyavijaya, Āgama Prabhākara Muni: Catalogue of Palm-leaf Manuscripts in the Śāntinātha Jain Bhaṇḍāra, Cambay, II. Baroda 1966. In: OLZ 64. 1969, Sp. 279-280.
150. Olschak, B. C.: Sikkim. Himalajastaat zwischen Gletschern und Dschungeln. Zürich 1965. In: ZDMG 120. 1970, S. 411-412.
151. Annual Bibliography of Indian Archaeology. Vol. XVIII for the years 1958-1960; Vol. XIX for the year 1961; Vol. XX for the years 1962-1963. Leiden 1964, 1965, 1966. In: OLZ 68. 1973, Sp. 176-177.

3. OBITUARIES

152. Hermann Jacobi †. „Frankfurter Zeitung", Reichsausgabe. Mittwoch, den 27. Oktober 1937, Nr. 547-548, S. 10.

III. EDITORIAL ACTIVITY

New Indian Antiquary 2. 1939. Mitherausgeber von No. 1-3.

H. Lüders, Varuṇa. Aus dem Nachlaß herausgegeben von L. Alsdorf. I: Varuṇa und die Wasser. Göttingen 1951. VIII, 337 S.

Indo-Iranian Journal. Mitglied des Editorial Board Vol. I ff. 1957 ff.

H. Lüders. Varuṇa. Aus dem Nachlaβ herausgegeben von L. Alsdorf. II: Varuṇa und das Ṛta. Göttingen 1959. XXIII, 427 S.

A Critical Pāli Dictionary. Begun by V. Treckner. Vol. II. Continuing the Work of Dines Andersen and Helmer Smith. Kopenhagen: Munksgaard in Komm. 1968 ff.Editor-in-Chief Fasc. 5 ff.

IV. ARTICLES ON LUDWIG ALSDORF

Indo-Iranian Journal, Vol. 20, Nos. 3/4. 1978, pp. 339-342 (by Gustav Roth).

Zeitschrift der Deutschen Morgenländischen Gesellschaft, Bd. 129, 1. 1979, pp. 1-7 (by Klaus Bruhn).

Sambodhi, Vol. 6, Nos. 3-4. 1978, pp. 77-78.

Journal of the Oriental Institute, Vol. 27, Nos. 3-4. 1978, pp. 131-133 (by A. N. Jani).

Almanach der Österreichischen Akademie der Wissenschaften, 129. Jahrgang. 1979, pp. 369-377 (by Gerhard Oberhammer).

A Critical Pāli Dictionary, Vol. II, Fasc. 11, Copenhagen 1981. pp. XV-XVII (by K. R. Norman).

V. ADDENDA

153. Indien in der Weltpolitik. Nationalsozialistische Monatshefte 11, 1940, pp. 764-775.
154. Das Spiel gegen den indischen Nationalismus. Das XX. Jahrhundert (Jena) 4. 1942, pp. 255-263.
    Herbert Hörhager, Die Volkstumsgrundlagen der indischen Nordwest-Grenzprovinz. Mit einer Kartenskizze. (Indien-Arbeiten Bd. 1).Heidelberg-Berlin-Magdeburg 1943.
155. Gujarati translation of Bibl. No. 30 by A. N. Jani (=Shri Mahavira Jaina Vidyalaya Golden Jubilee Volume Pt. I), Bombay 1968, Gujarātī Vibhāga, pp. 237-260.
156. The Impious Brahman and the Pious Candāla, in: Buddhist Studies in Honour of I.B. Horner. Ed. by L. Cousins, A. Kunst, K. R. Norman. Dordrecht 1974, pp. 9-13.

157. Pali miscellanies: uddhaṃsarā, in: Studien zur Indologie und Iranistik, 1. 1975, pp. 109-117.
A Critical Pāli Dictionary. Begun by V. Trenckner, Vol. II, Fascicle 9, Editor-in-Chief: L. Alsdorf. The Royal Danish Academy of Sciences and Letters, Copenhagen 1975.
158. Zwei Proben der Volksdichtung aus dem alten Magadha. Beiträge zur Indienforschung, Bd. 4. 1977, Ernst Waldschmidt zum 80. Geburtstag. Veröffentlichungen des Museums für Indische Kunst, Berlin 1977, pp. 17-24.
159. Das Bhūridatta-Jātaka. Ein antibrahmanischer Nāga-Roman. WZKS 21. 1977, pp. 25-55.
160. Jaina exegetical literature and the history of the Jaina Canon, in: Mahāvīra and His Teaching. [Editorial Board:] A. N. Upadhye [u.a.], Bombay 1977, pp. 1-8.
A Critical Pāli Dictionary. Begun by V. Trenckner, Vol. II, Fascicle 10, Editor-in-Chief: L. Alsdorf †. The Royal Danish Academy of Sciences and Letters, Copenhagen 1979.
161. Ardha-Māgadhī, in: The Language of the Earliest Buddhist Tradition, pp. 17-23 (=Symposien zur Buddhismusforschung, II. in: Abh. d. Ak. d. Wiss. in Göttingen, Göttingen 1980).

PROF. K. BRUHN (BERLIN)

CHRONOLOGY OF THE WRITINGS OF LUDWIG ALSDORF*

1928	Bibl. No. 1.
1929	(Review:) Bibl. No. 91.
1933	Bibl. Nos. 48, 59.
1935	Bibl. No. 49. —— (Reviews:) Bibl. Nos. 92-95.
1936	2. —— 96-97.
1937	3, 20, 52, 60, 152. —— 98-100.
1938	21-23, 43. —— 101-104.
1939	24, 87. —— 105-106.
1940	4, 153. —— 107-109.
1941	51.
1942	5, 6, 50, 63, 64, 154. —— 110-111.
1943	7, 58. —— 112-113.
1944	65.
1947	25.
1950	55, 66.
1951	15, 26, 53, 67. —— (Edited by L. Alsdorf:) Varuṇa I.
1952	8, 68, 81. —— 114-118.
1953	(Reviews:) 119-120.
1954	27, 82, 88. —— 121-125.
1955	9, 28, 35, 54, 69, 70, 71, 76, 83. —— 126-127.
1956	56, 57, 72, 73, 84, 89.
1957	29, 36, 85. —— 128-133.
1958	30. —— 134-136.
1959	37, 44, 86. —— (Ed.:) Varuṇa II. —— (Reviews:) 137-138.
1960	45, 46, 77. —— 139-141.
1961	16, 38, 61, 62, 74, 75, 78. —— 142.
1962	10, 11, 17, 31, 32, 79.
1963	(Review:) 143.
1964	18, 80. —— 144-146.

*The references are to the "Bibliography" (cf. pp. 15-32 ff.)

1965	(Review:) 147.
1966	12, 13, 39. —— 148.
1968	14, 40, 47, 155. — (Ed.:) CPD II 5.
1969	41. —— 149.
1970	(Ed.:) CPD II 6. — 150.
1971	19, 42, 90. —— (Ed.:) CPD II 7.
1972	90 *bis*.
1973	33, 34. —— (Ed.:) CPD II 8. —— 151.
1974	156.
1975	157. —— (Ed.:) CPD II 9.
1977	158-160.
1979	(Ed.:) CPD II 10.
1980	161.

R. P. Das (Hamburg)

BIBLIOGRAPHY OF REVIEWS OF LUDWIG ALSDORF'S INDEPENDENT PUBLICATIONS

Der Kumārapālapratibodha (1928, Bibl. no. 1)
Acta Orientalia 8. 1930, p. 79 (S. Konow)
The Indian Antiquary 59. 1930, p. 147-148 (J. Charpentier)
Indogermanische Forschungen 50. 1932, p. 250-251 (W. Wüst)
The Journal of the Royal Asiatic Society of Great Britain and Ireland 1930, p. 448-449 (L.D. Barnett)
*Orientalistische Literaturzeitung 33. 1930, col. 672-674 (C. Krause) Wiener Zeitschrift für die Kunde des Morgenlandes 43. 1936, p. 316-317 (E. Frauwallner)

Harivaṃśapurāṇa (1936, Bibl. no. 2)
Deutsche Literaturzeitung 58. 1937, col. 608-611 (J. Nobel)
The Journal of the Royal Asiatic Society of Great Britain and Ireland 1938, p. 600 (E.H. Johnston)
Literarisches Zentralblatt für Deutschland 87. 1936, col. 1110 (A. Paust)
Orientalistische Literaturzeitung 40. 1937, col. 753-756 (H. Losch)
Oriental Literary Digest 1, 3. 1937, col. 7-8 (A.M. Ghatage)
Wiener Zeitschrift für die Kunde des Morgenlandes 44. 1937, p. 317-318 (E. Frauwallner)
Zeitschrift der Deutschen Morgenländischen Gesellschaft 90. 1936, p. 726-727 (W. Printz)

Apabhraṃśa-Studien (1937, Bibl. no. 3)
*Bulletin de la Société de Linguistique de Paris 38. 1937, 114, p. 52-53 (J. Bloch)
Orientalistische Literaturzeitung 42. 1939, col. 245-248 (H. Losch)
*Oriental Literary Digest 1, 8. 1938, col. 4-5 (A.M. Ghatage)
Zeitschrift der Deutschen Morgenländischen Gesellschaft 91. 1937, p. 767 (W. Printz)

Indien (1940, Bibl. no. 4).
Anthropos 37-40. 1942-1945, p. 416-417 (W. Koppers)

Archiv für Wanderungswesen und Auslandkunde 13. 1942/1943, p. 118
Beiblatt zur Anglia 52. 1941, p. 183-185 (W. Fischer)
Beiblatt zur Anglia 53. 1942, p. 95 (W. Fischer)
Berliner Monatshefte 19. 1941, p. 679-681 (F. Ernst)
Die Bücherei 8. 1941, p. 297-298 (K. Hecker)
Bücherkunde 8. 1941, p. 130 (K. Rüdiger)
Cahiers Franco-Allemands 9. 1942, p. 133 (J. Renaurd)
Deutsche Allgemeine Zeitung 20. 1941, 199/200 (27.4.1941), Literarische Rundschau (H. Büchsenschütz)
Deutsche Literaturzeitung 63. 1942, col. 10-13 (J. Nobel)
Deutsche Monatshefte in Norwegen 2.1941, 9/10, p. 37-39 (E. Hilck)
Geographischer Anzeiger 42. 1941, p. 358 (N. Krebs)
Geographisches Jahrbuch 61. 1954, p. 28 (E. Reiner)
Geographische Zeitschrift 49. 1943, p. 155 (E. Weigt)
Großdeutsches Leihbüchereiblatt 3. 1941, p. 253-254 (W. Fensterer)
Kölnische Volkszeitung 82. 1941, 111 (22.4.1941), p. 3 (B. Spuler)
Literarisches Zentralblatt für Deutschland 92. 1941, col. 279 (K. Roepke)
Luftwelt 9. 1942, p. 258-259 (A. Juhre)
Marine Rundschau 47. 1942, p. 260
Monatshefte für Auswärtige Politik 8. 1941, p. 593
Nationalsozialistische Monatshefte 12. 1941, p. 635 (K. Rüdiger)
Die Neue Literatur 42. 1941, p. 299 (W. Vesper)
Orientalistische Literaturzeitung 45. 1942, col. 133-134 (H. von Glasenapp)
Orientalistische Literaturzeitung 47. 1944, col. 144 (H. von Glasenapp)
Petermanns Geographische Mitteilungen 88. 1942, p. 228 (K. Haushofer)
Schule der Freiheit 9. 1941-1942, p. 258 (K. Becker)
Die Welt des Islams 23. 1941, p. 202-204 (G. Jäschke)
Die Weltliteratur 17. 1942, p. 43 (E. Klingmüller)
Wiener Zeitschrift für die Kunde des Morgenlandes 49. 1942, p. 158-159 (H. Günther)
Wille und Macht 10. 1942, 8, p. 40 (Kaspar)
Zeitschrift der Deutschen Morgenländischen Gesellschaft 96. 1942, p. 156-157 (K. Fischer)

Zeitschrift der Gesellschaft für Erdkunde zu Berlin 1943, p. 270 (J. März)
Zeitschrift für Erdkunde 9. 1941, p. 575 (K. Helbig)
Zeitschrift für Geopolitik 19. 1942, p. 105-106 (K. Haushofer)

Deutsch-Indische Geistesbeziehungen. (1942, Bibl. no. 6)
Archiv für Wanderungswesen und Auslandkunde 13. 1942/1943, p. 118
Auswärtige Politik 9. 1942, p. 1040-1041 (Voigtländer)
Auswärtige Politik 10. 1943, p. 296 (Lehmann)
Beiblatt zur Anglia 54/55. 1943/1944, p. 42-45 (W. Fischer)
Berliner Monatshefte 20. 1942. p. 517 (F. Olshausen)
Bibliographie des Deutschtums im Ausland 7. 1943, p. 56 (G. Widmann)
Die Bücherei 10. 1943, p. 311 (T. Steche)
Bücherkunde 10. 1943, p. 196
Forschungsdienst 15. 1943, Schrifttum, p. 33 (Lorch)
Geistige Arbeit 10. 1943, 8-14, p. 3 (R.F. Merkel)
Geographischer Anzeiger 44. 1943, p. 334 (H.F. Zeck)
Geographisches Jahrbuch 61. 1954, p. 138 (E. Reiner)
Geographische Zeitschrift 49. 1943, p. 281-282 (N. Krebs)
Internationale Zeitschrift für Erziehung 12. 1943, p. 90 (T. Wilhelm)
Marine Rundschau 47. 1942, p. 949-950
Mitteilungen der Geographischen Gesellschaft Wien 86. 1943, p. 303 (E. Reisick)
Mitteilungsblatt des NSLB, Gauwaltung Sudetenland 1943, 2, p. 16 (K. Zepnik)
Nationalsozialistische Monatshefte 14.1943, p. 434 (S. Zantke)
Die Neue Literatur 44. 1943, p. 38 (J. Oven)
Orientalistische Literaturzeitung 46. 1943, col. 474 (F.O. Schrader)
Petermanns Geographische Mitteilungen 89. 1943, p. 111-112 (K. Helbig)
Wirtschaftsdienst 28. 1943, p. 248 (M.K.)
Wissen und Wehr 24. 1943, p. 111 (F. Olshausen)
Die Woche 44. 1942, 42 (21.10.1942), p. 20 (Lewalter)
Zeitschrift der Gesellschaft für Erdkunde zu Berlin 1943, p. 185 (J. März)
Zeitschrift für Erdkunde 11. 1943, p. 217 (W. Schneefuß)
Zeitschrift für Geopolitik 19. 1942, p. 516-517 (K. Haushofer)

Indien und Ceylon (1943, Bibl. no. 7).
Berliner Monatshefte 22. 1944, p. 205 (F. Olshausen)
Geographischer Anzeiger 45. 1944, p. 284 (H.F. Zeck)
Petermanns Geographische Mitteilungen 90. 1944, p. 295 (K. Helbig)
Die Welt des Islams N.S. 1. 1951, p. 310-311 (G. Jäschke)
Zeitschrift der Deutschen Morgenländischen Gesellschaft 98. 1944, p. 415 (H. Scheel)

Geschichte Asicns (1950, Bibl. no. 55)
Acta Orientalia 21. 1953, p. 153 (K. Grønbech)
The American Historical Review 56. 1950-1951, p. 894-895 (H.G. Callis)
Archiv Orientální 22. 1954, p. 134-136 (V. Gampert)
Außenpolitik 3. 1952, p. 834-835 (H. Gottschalk)
Buchanzeiger für öffentliche Büchereien 8. 1955, 90/91, p. 15 (W. Bayer)
Bücherei und Bildung 7. 1955, B, p. 660-661 (W. Bayer)
Bücherschiff 2. 1952, 12, p. 4-5 (F.G.)
Erasmus 4. 1951, col. 45-48 (O.F. de Battaglia)
Das ganze Deutschland (Deutsche Kommentare) 3. 1951, 1 (1.1.1951), p. 4 (W. Schwarz)
Geschichte in Wissenschaft und Unterricht 1. 1950, p. 508-509 (H. Franke)
Historische Zeitschrift 177. 1954, p. 158-161 (E. Schmitt)
Orientalistische Literaturzeitung 53. 1958, col. 203-207 (R. Heine-Geldern)
Oriente Moderno 34. 1954, p. 196 (E. Rossi)
Pacific Affairs 24. 1951, p. 190-194 (W. Eberhard)
Tribus 1. 1951, p. 249-251 (H. Rau)
Universitas 6. 1951, p. 207-208 (A. Eckardt)
Welt und Wort 5. 1950, p. 444 (F. Dirlmeier)
Die Zeit 6. 1951, 34 (23.8.1951), p. 12

(Ed.:) H. Lüders, *Varuṇa I* (1951).
Acta Orientalia 22. 1955, p. 82 (G. Morgenstierne)
*Deutsche Literaturzeitung 74. 1953, col. 400-405 (H. Lommel) [Reprinted: Herman Lommel. Kleine Schriften herausgegeben von Klaus L. Janert. Wiesbaden: Steiner 1978. (Glasenapp-Stiftung 16), p. 591-594.]

East and West 4. 1953-1954, p. 127 (R. Gnoli)
*Erasmus 5. 1952, col. 362-365 (L. Renou)
The Indo-Asian Culture 3. 1954, p. 298 (J.C. Tavadia)
Indogermanische Forschungen 63. 1957/58, p. 288-290 (R. Birwé)
Journal Asiatique 240. 1952, p. 114-116 (L. Renou)
Journal of the Asiatic Society of Bengal (4th S.) 1. 1959, p. 267-269 (B. Banerjee)
The Journal of the Royal Asiatic Society of Great Britain and Ireland 1954. p. 85-86 (T. Burrow)
Oriens 6. 1953, p. 386-387 (J. Gonda)
*Orientalistische Literaturzeitung 49. 1954, col. 389-395 (K. Hoffmann) [Reprinted: Karl Hoffmann. Aufsätze zur Indoiranistik herausgegeben von Johanna Narten. Wiesbaden: Reichert 1975, p. 46-51.]
*Zeitschrift der Deutschen Morgenländischen Gesellschaft 101. 1951, p. 407-418 (P. Thieme) [Reprinted: Paul Thieme. Kleine Schriften <herausgegeben von Georg Buddruss>. Wiesbaden: Steiner 1971. (Glasenapp-Stiftung 5), p. 642-653.]

Vorderindien (1955, Bibl. no. 9).
Annales. Economies, sociétés, civilisations 14. 1959, p. 591 (L. Dumont)
Asien-Bibliographie 7. 1955, 25, p. 16 (no. 105) (W. Exner?)
Atlantis 29. 1957, 9, p. [2] (Habbe)
Aufbau (New York) 24. 1958, 7 (14.2.1958), p. 18 (m.g.)
Der Außenhandelskaufmann 1959, p. 420 (=03 022)
Bayerischer Rundfunk 22.11.1955, Chronik des Tages (21.00-21.30 h.) (H.-J. Netzer)
Bayerisches Sonntagsblatt für die katholische Familie 74. 1955, 45(6.11.1955), p. 12
Die Berufsbildende Schule 10. 1958, p. 60 (Plypiak)
Bibliographie Géographique Internationale 1954-1955, p. 497 (M.C. Robequain)
Bibliographie mensuelle. Bibliothèque de la Société de Géographie, Paris 9. 1957, 6, p. 2
Bollettino della Societa' Geografica Italiana 10. 1957, p. 241-242 (R. Riccardi)
Braunschweigerisches Industrie- und Handelsblatt 1956, p. 213
Braunschweiger Nachrichten 3. 1955, 201 (31.8.1955), p. 6 (wk)

Buchanzeiger für öffentliche Büchereien 11.1958, 119, p. 10 (M.F. Wocke)
Bücherei und Bildung 10.1958, B, p. 150 (M.F. Wocke)
Bücher für die Wirtschaft 2. 1956, p. 3 (ss)
Bücherschiff 6. 1956, 7, p. 7
Christ und Welt 10. 1957, 24 (13.6.1957), p. 15 (G.W.)
Contact International 6. 1956, 7, p. 11 (H. Adamietz)
Deutsche Kommentare 7. 1955, 51 (17.12.1955), p. 6 (G.J. Roos)
Deutsche Literaturzeitung 78. 1957, col. 149-150 (R. Hauschild)
Deutscher Forschungsdienst 2. 1956, 27 (3.7. 1956), p. 3
Deutsch-Indische Studiengesellschaft e. V., Mitteilungsblatt 10. Juli 1955, p. 51
Deutsch-Indische Studiengesellschaft e.V., Mitteilungsblatt 11. Dezember 1955, p. 59-60 (H. Lehmann)
Echo der Zeit (Recklinghausen) [5]. 1956, 30 (22.6.1956), p. 11
*Erasmus 11.1958, col. 618-619 (R.N. Dandekar)
Die Erde 8. 1956, p. 85-86 (E. Weigt)
Erdkunde 10. 1956, p. 252 (K. Helbig)
Europa Archiv 10. 1955, p. 8371
Frankfurter Neue Presse 10. 1955, 271 (22.11.1956), Vorausgabe, p. 3 (H. Hanisch)
Freiheit (Tel-Aviv) 5. 1956, 6 (15.6.1956), p. 15 (G.Z. Barth)
Gelesen — Bedacht — Erfahren. Mitteilungen des Vereins für das Büchereiwesen in Schleswig-Holstein e. V., Bücherbrief 2, Mai 1957, p. 15
Geografisk Tidsskrift 56. 1957, p. 151-152 (K.M. Jensen)
Geographica Helvetica 10. 1955, p. 180 (H. Gutersohn)
The Geographical Journal 122. 1956, p. 123 (G.R.C.)
*The Geographical Review 47. 1957, p. 149-150 (J.E. Spencer)
Geographische Rundschau 7. 1955, p. 411-412 (H. Steche)
Hamburger Abendblatt 8. 1955, 281 (2.12.1955), p. 13
Hamburgisches Welt-Wirtschafts-Archiv, Bibliographischer Wochenbericht 1955, 39 (30.9.1955), p. 6
Hessische Nachrichten 11. 1955, 292 (16.12.1955), p. 3
Das Historisch-Politische Buch 4. 1956, p. 156-157 (H. Lehmann)
The Indo-Asian Culture 5. 1956, p. 123-124 (K.H. Buschmann)
Institut für Auslandsbeziehungen, Stuttgart, Mitteilungen 6. 1956, p. 191 (Bi)
Die katholischen Missionen 75. 1956, p. 34
Die katholische Schule [2]. 1956, 23 (3.12.1956), p. 14

Kosmos 52. 1956, p. XL (W. Böckler)
Kulturgeografi 3. 1955-1957, p. 80 (J. Humlum)
Kultus und Unterricht 6. 1957, Nichtamtlicher Teil, p. 93-94
Literaturanzeiger für das allgemeine wissenschaftliche Schrifttum/ Auswahlbericht 5. 1955, 2, p. 14
Mitteilungen der Fränkischen Geographischen Gesellschaft 2. 1955, p. 186 (W. Kucher)
Mitteilungen der Geographischen Gesellschaft, Wien 98. 1956, p. 266-267 (J. Weichinger)
Mitteilungen der Pädagogischen Arbeitsstätte München 7. 1956, 11 (27.2.1956), p. [3]
Das Neue Buch 1. 1955/1956, p. 270
Neue politische Literatur 1. 1956, col. 230-231 (W.E. Mühlmann)
Das Neueste 1955, 5, no. 345
Österreichische Neue Tageszeitung 1959, 244 (21.10.1959), p. 4 (H.Z.)
Orientalistische Literaturzeitung 53. 1958, col. 160-162 (W. Kirfel)
Das Parlament 11. 1961, 33/34 (16.8.1961), p. 23 (H. Adamietz)
Petermanns Geographische Mitteilungen 100. 1956, p. 220 (E. Reiner)
Radio Station WEVD, New York 7.5.1957, German Literature Hour, Radio Book Review 4/27/1957 (P.M. Lindt)
Revue Francaise de Science Politique 6. 1956, p. 249
Rheinische Post 10. 1955, 210 (10.9.1955), p. [26] (E. Vietta)
Schwäbisches Tagblatt 12.1956, 149 (30.6.1956), p. [6] (wn)
Scientia 93. 1958, p. 116 (R. Almagià)
Staats-Zeitung und Herold (Woodside, Broadway, New York) 109. 1957, 22 (2.6.1957), Sektion C, p. 14 (g.)
Steinlach-Bote 12. 1956, 149 (30.6.1956), p. [6] (wn)
Stuttgarter Zeitung 12. 1956, 173 (28.7.1956), p. 34 (H. Koester)
Süddeutscher Rundfunk 24.3.1957, Meinungen zum Zeitgeschehen (19. 15-19.30 h.) (P. Eckart)
Südkurier 13. 1957, 16 (19/20.1.1957), p. 18
Svensk Geografisk Årsbok 31. 1955, p. 276 (E. Wester)
Telegraf (Berlin) 11. 1956, 101 (29.4.1956), Literatur der Zeit, p. [2] (H. Gensecke)
Tijdschrift voor Economische en Sociale Geografie 47. 1956, p. 83 (G. de Jong)
Tijdschrift voor Economische en Sociale Geografie 49. 1958, p. 155-156 (J.J. Hanrath)

Übersee-Rundschau 1955, 9, p. 34 (K. Helbig)
Die Welt 11. 1956, 193 (18.8.1956), p. [34] (K. Ch.)
Westdeutscher Rundfunk 25.5.1956, Politische Literatur (14.00-14.15 h.) (K.-H. Weigel)
Westermanns Monatshefte 96. 1955, 6, p. 101-102 (W. Tietze)
Wirtschaftsdienst 36. 1956, p. 58
Ymer 75. 1955, p. 288 (G. Walldén)
Zeitnahe Schularbeit 11. 1958, p. 322
Zeitungs-Verlag und Zeitschriften-Verlag 53. 1956, p. 538

(Ed.:) H. Lüders, *Varuṇa II* (1959).
Oriens 13-14. 1961, p. 398-410 (J. Gonda)
*Zeitschrift der Deutschen Morgenländischen Gesellschaft 113. 1963, p. 683-694 (P. Thieme) [Reprinted: Paul Thieme. Kleine Schriften <herausgegeben von Georg Buddruss>. Wiesbaden: Steiner 1971. (Glasenapp-Stiftung 5), p. 777-788.]

Vegetarismus und Rinderverehrung (1962, Bibl. no. 10).
Bulletin of the School of Oriental and African Studies, University of London 27. 1964, p. 231 (J.G. de Casparis)
*Indo-Iranian Journal 9. 1965-1966, p. 147-149 (J.C. Heesterman)
Oriens 17. 1964. p. 270-276 (F. László)
Orientalistische Literaturzeitung 60. 1965, col. 186-188 (H. Losch)
Zeitschrift der Deutschen Morgenländischen Gesellschaft 113. 1963, p. 385-386 (J.F. Sprockhoff)

Aśokas Separatedikte von Dhauli und Jaugaḍa (1962, Bibl. no. 11)
Journal of the American Oriental Society 83. 1963, p. 379-380 (L.A. Schwarzschild)
Oriens 18-19. 1967, p. 392-293 (W. Kirfel)
Orientalistische Literaturzeitung 60. 1965, col. 507-509 (U. Schneider)

The Āryā Stanzas of the Uttarajhāyā (1966, Bibl. no. 12)
Bulletin of the School of Oriental and African Studies, University of London 30. 1967, p. 247-248 (J.C. Wright)
*Journal Asiatique 256. 1968, p. 147-149 (C. Caillat)
Orientalistische Literaturzeitung 65. 1970, col. 495-497 (G. Roth)
Wiener Zeitschrift für die Kunde Süd- und Ostasiens und Archiv für indische Philosophie 11. 1967, p. 214-215 (E. Frauwallner)

Zeitschrift der Deutschen Morgenländischen Gesellschaft 122. 1972, p. 431-433 (K. Bruhn)

Les études jaina (1966, Bibl. No. 13).
* Indo-Iranian Journal 13. 1971, p. 207-210 (J.W. de Jong) [Reprinted: Buddhist Studies by J.W. de Jong, edited by Gregory Schopen. Berkeley, California: Asian Humanities Press 1979, p. 213-216.]
*Journal Asiatique 256.1968, p. 145-147 (C. Caillat)

Die Āryā-Strophen des Pāli-Kanons (1968, Bibl. No. 14)
Bulletin de la Société de Linguistique de Paris 64.1969, 2, p. 22-23 C. (Caillat)
*Indo-Iranian Journal 13.1971, p. 210-212 (J. W. de Jong) [Reprinted: Buddhist Studies by J.W. de Jong, edited by Gregory Schopen. Berkeley, California: Asian Humanities Press 1979, p. 216-218.]
Journal of the American Oriental Society 90.1970, p. 586-587 (L.A. Schwarzschild)
Orientalistische Literaturzeitung 68.1973, col. 280-281 (H. Kopp)

(Ed.:) (*A Critical Pāli Dictionary II 5-10* (1968-79)
Annals of the Bhandarkar Oriental Research Institute 56.1975, p. 251 (P.V. Bapat) (Fasc. 8)
Annals of the Bhandarkar Oriental Research Institute 64.1983, p. 285-287 (J.R. Joshi) (Fasc. 10)
Bulletin de la Société de Linguistique de Paris 68.1973, 2, p. 112-114 (C. Caillat) (Fasc. 7)
Indogermanische Forschungen 75.1970, p. 299-303 (C. Caillat) (Fasc. 5)
Indogermanische Forschungen 78.1973, p. 247-249 (C. Caillat) (Fasc. 7)
Indogermanische Forschungen 79.1974, p. 250-252 and 252-255 (C. Caillat) (Fasc. 6 and 8)
Indogermanische Forschungen 81.1976, p. 327-329 (C. Caillat) (Fasc. 9)
Indogermanische Forschungen 88.1983, p. 312-318 (C. Caillat) (Fasc. 10)
Indo-Iranian Journal 14.1972, p. 102-103 (T. Rajapatirana) (Fasc. 5)

Indo-Iranian Journal 18.1976, p. 140 (T. Rajapatirana) (Fasc. 8)

Indo-Iranian Journal 19.1977, p. 116 (T. Rajapatirana) (Fasc. 6-7)

Journal Asiatique 264.1976, p. 480-481 (J.-C. Coppieters) (Fasc. 6-8)

Journal of the American Oriental Society 90.1970, p. 408-409 (L.A. Schwarzschild) (Fasc. 5)

Journal of the American Oriental Society 93.1973, p. 376-377 (L.A. Schwarzschild) (Fasc. 6)

Journal of the American Oriental Society 95.1975, p. 153-154 (L.A. Schwarzschild) (Fasc. 7)

Journal of the American Oriental Society 96.1976, p. 460-461 (L.A. Schwarzschild) (Fasc. 8)

Journal of the American Oriental Society 99.1979, p. 517 (L.A. Schwarzschild) (Fasc. 9)

The Journal of the Royal Asiatic Society of Great Britain and Ireland 1977, p. 127-128 (K.R. Norman) (Fasc. 9)

Orientalistische Literaturzeitung 69.1974, col. 493-494 (P. Horsch) (Fasc. 6)

Orientalistische Literaturzeitung 74.1979, col. 391-394 and 493-495 (K.R. Norman) (Fasc. 7-8 and 9)

Orientalistische Literaturzeitung 77.1982, col. 402-404 (K.R. Norman) (Fasc. 10)

Wiener Zeitschrift für die Kunde Süd- und Ostasiens und Archiv für indische Philosophie 14.1970, p. 210 (E. Frauwallner) (Fasc. 5)

Zeitschrift für Vergleichende Sprachforschung 84.1970, p. 177-186 (O. von Hinüber) (Fasc. 5)

Zeitschrift für Vergleichende Sprachforschung 94.1980, p. 10-31 (O. von Hinüber) (Fasc. 6-10)

LUDWIG ALSDORF'S OEUVRE—REVIEWS REPRINTED

JULES BLOCH

L. ALSDORF.—*Apabhraṃśa-Studien* (Abhandlungen f.d. Kunde des Morgenlandes XXII.2). Leipzig, Deutsche Morgenländische Gesellschaft, in komm. bei Brockhaus, 1937, in-8, viii-113 p.

Ce petit livre apporte un progrès important à la connaissance du conglomérat de dialectes littéraires médiévaux que la tradition réunit sous le nom d'apabhraṃca. Les textes et les grammaires indigènes en fournissaient une image confuse et incohérente au point qu'un linguiste prudent et soucieux de réalité répugnait à y reconnaitre des documents. Les recherches de M. Alsdorf y apportent plus d'ordre et de clarté, par suite plus de réalité.

Elles reposent d'abord sur une revision minutieuse des strophes isolées rassemblées par Pischel dans ses *Materialien*, et dont une réédition partielle est donnée dans les 40 dernières pages du volume présenté ici; et sur la comparaison avec des textes étendus publiés antérieurement par Jacobi et par M. Alsdorf lui-même. Il a également essayé de mettre en ordre la métrique, moyen de contrôle essentiel à l'établissement des textes et donc à la vérification des formes (p. 39-56; oserai-je signaler que *dohā*, nom d'une strophe, est du genre masculin?). Cela lui permet de nettoyer tout de suite et définitivement la grammaire de certaines notions fausses, qui embrouillaient l'aspect de la langue: il n'y a pas de génitif sans désinence, ni de passif à sens actif (p. 56-68).

La première partie, p. 5-37, est consacrée à l'examen de problèmes de morphologie et de phonétique qui se commandent les uns les autres. Ici il reste des points litigieux, par exemple le traitement *asma*>*ahā*—qui il est vrai n'est guère plus étonnant que le traitement généralement admis *-asya*> *-ahu*. Mais il y a des gains certains, comme p. 31, le rejet de mon hypothèse sur la désinence de 1re p. pluriel, à laquelle la chronologie s'oppose; ou probables, comme l'admission de contractions vocaliques de type moderne. Surtout on fait enfin la distinction nécessaire entre les strophes des *Materialien*, les *deux* catégories de textes jaina, enfin les citations du Prākṛtapingala et à plus forte raison les textes bouddhiques. Et en ce qui concerne Hemacandra, il est établi que ses citations contiennent des modernismes; certains méme s'accordent avec l'hindi oriental: conclusion inattendue, que l'histoire des textes expliquera sans doute un jour, M. Alsdorf aidant.

C. Caillet

Ludwig ALSDORF. *Les études jaina.* État présent et tâches futures. Conférences.—[Paris], Collège de France, 1965; 97 pages 20 × 13.

The Āryā Stanzas of the Uttarajjhāyā. Contributions to the Text History and Interpretation of a Canonical Jaina Text (Abh. der Geistes- und Sozialwissenschaftlichen Klasse 1966. Nr. 2. Akademie der Wissenchaften und der Literatur in Mainz, 68 p.).

Les nombreux documents laissés par les jaina n'ont pas seulement une valeur intrinsèque. Leur exploitation qui, parfois, a servi le progrès de la bouddhologie, est naturellement indispensable si l'on veut établir l'histoire de la pensée et de la philosophie indiennes, et, plus encore peut-être, pour retracer le développement linguistique de l'indo-aryen. Il est donc très regrettable que les études jaina aient si peu retenu les savants occidentaux. Quelques-uns seulement s'y sont intéressés, qui, pour la plupart, appartiennent à l'école allemande: ils ont mené à bien des travaux à tous égards remarquables, et fondé une tradition qui, de Georg Bühler et Albrecht Weber, en passant par Hermann Jacobi et le Suisse Ernst Leumann, s'est transmise à Walther Schubring et à Ludwig Alsdorf. Ce dernier est aujourd'hui professeur à l'Université de Hambourg, où il dirige le Seminar für Kultur und Geschichte Indiens, l'un des rares instituts occidentaux où se poursuivent les recherches sur le jinisme. Invité au Collège de France aux mois de mars et avril 1965, il y a fait le point des études jaina. Le recueil de ces conférences forme un opuscule extrêmement précieux.

On trouvera dans la première le rappel des discussions relatives à la langue du canon śvetāmbara. Elève de Lüders, et considérant comme désormais prouvé que les textes les plus anciens du canon bouddhique pāli ont été traduits d'un vieux prākrit oriental (p. 15), M.A. admet qu'un processus similaire a eu lieu dans le cas des jaina : il tient leur canon pour la transposition occidentale de textes primitivement composés en une authentique "ardha-māgadhī", et les *Études jaina* citent des fragments d'un commentaire ancien, l'*Uttarādhyayana-Niryukti*, qui, présentant *l* pour *r*, et des nominatifs singuliers masculins et neutres en *-e*, mais ignorant *ś*, ont en effet toutes les apparences du parler "semi-māgadhi" (24).

Les conférences suivantes tracent pour l'avenir un programme détaillé. La tâche la plus urgente, considérable à vrai dire, sera de constituer l'édition critique du canon jaina. Le travail est amorcé. W. Schubring a établi et publié, exemplairement, le texte des plus anciens *Chedasūtra*, et, au reste, nous disposons d'une "base critique suffisante pour la réalisation de ce qu'on pourrait appeler une vulgate", car il ne manque pas d'éditions indiennes, et elles ont chacune à peu prés "la valeur d'un bon manuscrit" (31). Certaines, ainsi celles des Sthānakvāsin, offrent en outre diverses particularités instructives. Enfin les anciens commentaires nous deviennent peu à peu accessibles grâce au zèle de plusieurs érudits jaina contemporains: M.A. en souligne l'utilité, tout en marquant les limites de "la valeur de la tradition jaina pour la compréhension du canon" (37 et suiv.). Il conviendra de ne pas trop tarder à publier une concordance des passages versifiés, tâche dont l'ampleur ne doit pas étre tenue pour excessive. Quant aux digambara, qui longtemps avaient répugné à ouvrir leurs bibliothèques, ils diffusent aujourd'hui leur tradition avec diligence et bonheur: nous devrons l'étudier, reconnaître son originalité. Il faudra en outre comparer systématiquement les documents des deux églises, digambara et śvetāmbara (85 et suiv.).

Les travaux de critique textuelle et de compréhension linguistique auront frayé la voie en vue d'une "critique supérieure" qui permettra de "déterminer l'histoire et les rapports réciproques des textes, de disjoindre les conglomérats de parties d'âges différents" (47): analyse d'autant plus souhaitable que Mahāvīra paraît être l'un des penseurs les plus originaux de l'antiquité indienne. Pour la mener à bien, M.A. recommande d'utiliser avec toutes les ressources de la philologie traditionnelle, l'outil si exact qu'est la métrique. On pourra voir sa méthode appliquée au cours de la quatrième conférence où sont considérés plusieurs chapitres de l'*Uttarādhyayana*.

La troisième, cependant, reprend après d'autres savants l'étude de l'*āryā*. Les observations et les déductions présentées par M.A. intéressent la philologie indienne tout entière. Il examine comparativement l'occurrence de ce mètre subtil dans la littérature bouddhique pālie et dans la littérature prākrite des jaina. L'āryā de type ancien n'est nulle part attestée en abondance. Au contraire, le type récent devient très vite le mètre banal des jaina quand ils composent en prākrit. Or, M.A. ne relève d'āryā que dans quelque 450 strophes des Écritures pālies canoniques, et il n'est pas rare qu'elles aient été déformées, voire dénaturées. D'où la conclusion de M.A.: l'āryā nouvelle était née dès avant le IIIe siècle av. J.-C., bien plus tôt que ne l'a cru Ernst Leumann; mais, tandis que, de toute évidence, ce mètre connaissait une très grande vogue en Inde même, les bouddhistes singhalais eurent tôt fait d'en oublier les rythmes, et de revenir au śloka. Conclusion corroborée, en quelque sorte, par les deux exceptions que fournit la littérature pā. postcanonique: l'āryā est le mètre du *Nettipakaraṇa,* qu'on a d'autres raisons de supposer écrit sur le continent; elle se rencontre aussi en divers passages des oeuvres de Buddhaghośa, ce grand brahmane originaire de l'Inde du Nord. Comme, d'autre part, il est manifeste que, dans l'Inde, l'emploi de l'āryā est postérieur à celui du śloka, et surtout à celui des antiques triṣṭubh-jagatī, M.A. est fondé à admettre que la formule du credo bouddhique *ye dhammā* ... (de rythme āryā!) ne remonte pas aux origines de la Communauté. Inversement, tels fragments jaina en triṣṭubhjagatī seraient bien antérieurs au IIIe siècle: il se pourrait que les morceaux les plus anciens nous reportent, à très peu près, à l'époque de la prédication de Mahāvīra (71), qu'ils nous fassent entendre comme le lointain écho des Paroles du Maître. On voit comment une éblouissante étude technique conduit M. Alsdorf à des conclusions aussi fermes qu'émouvantes.

The *Āryā Stanzas of the Uttarajjhāyā* prolongent en quelque sorte la quatrième conférence des *Études jaina.* L'investigation métrique des chapitres retenus, dont le contenu est plutôt de tendance thèorique (*infra*), fournit à elle seule les indices irrécusables qui servent à établir solidement l'histoire textuelle, qui donc obligent à rèviser l'analyse littérale de ces exposés, et, par suite, dans une certaine mesure, leur interprétation.

M. Alsdorf semble avoir été intéressé à ces recherches par l'enseignement de son maître W. Schubring, auquel, précisément, sont dédiées les *Āryā Stanzas*. A plusieurs reprises, en effet, M.A. renvoie le lecteur aux pages où Schubring tout en présentant les *Worte Mahāvīras* (en 1926) traite de questions de prosodie dans le canon śvetāmbara (2 et suiv.). Le même savant avait d'ailleurs, dés 1910, admirablement mené l'analyse prosodique des *Bambhaceräiṃ* (cf. son *Ācārâṅgasūtra*, traduit dans les *Worte*, p. 66-121, sous le titre "Reines Leben"): hors des portions en prose, les rythmes récurrents dans ces vieux aphorismes sont ceux de la triṣṭubh et du śloka.

La présente étude porte sur une oeuvre à tous égards différente. Recueil ancien, l'*Uttar.* pourtant atteste déjà le recul de la triṣṭubh, utilise largement le śloka, et montre l'intrusion de l'āryā "récente" (cf. *Worte*, 3). Celle-ci n'est pas encore, comme elle va le devenir, le mètre dominant. Néanmoins, parmi les quatre sutta que Schubring a nommés les "seniors du Canon", l'*Uttar.* est celui qui offre le plus grand nombre de ces āryā nouvelles: 130 environ (nombre nécessairement approximatif, certaines stances étant mixtes, d'autres douteuses). Elles ont permis à M.A. de circonscrire clairement les différents morceaux hétérogènes qui ont constitué le texte canonique, de déterminer leur âge relatif et leurs relations mutuelles.

Il en distingue trois catégories: 1° celles qui ont été composées exclusivement *ad hoc,* pour remplacer tel développement originel en prose d'un chapitre initialement mixte (en prose et vers); 2° celles qui ont été grossièrement interpolées; 3° celles dont l'interpolation est plus subtile: ce sont cent neuf āryā relevées dans sept chapitres qui appartiennent au dernier tiers de l'*Uttar.*, et qui traitent de dogmatique et de discipline. M.A. a pu établir: *a.* que beaucoup figurent également dans des traités plus récents du Canon (46 ont été identifiées, et parfois les digambara en ont aussi une version): ce sont donc des développements d'école; *b.* que lusieurs ont été substituées à d'anciens śloka, ou qu'elles résultent du remaniement de ceux-ci; 4° que, dans un texte primitif composé en śloka, et porteur d'un enseignement relativement clair et simple, la plupart introduisent mécaniquement, parfois sans souci de la syntaxe locale, des matériaux évidemment hétérogènes: amplifications, réduplications, analyses scolastiques, listes de synonymes, énumérations mnémoniques, considérations techniques absconses comme il s'en rencontre couramment dans les niryukti et les commentaires en général. M.A. montre que la même méthode permet de mieux déceler quand et comment les jaina ont introduit dans leur propre doctrine des éléments qu'ils empruntaient à des sectes rivales.

Pour conclure ses analyses, il reconstruit le possible schéma originel de quelques-uns des adhyāya examinés: on pourrait y reconnaître comme des spécimens de cette ancienne poésie "śramanique" sur laquelle Winternitz et plusieurs érudits indiens ont attiré l'attention.

Considérées dans tous leurs détails, les conclusions auxquelles aboutit M.A. sont naturellement en partie hypothétiques, et il les présente lui-même comme telles. Mais elles se corroborent mutuellement pour ce qui est de l'essentiel. Ces études aideront les indianistes à mieux comprendre plusieurs chapitres de l'*Uttar.*, à mieux situer les différents niveaux de réflexion qui s'y expriment. et à prendre conscience de la considérable évolution à laquelle s'est prêtée une communauté que l'on s'est trop habitué à tenir pour immuable.

Il faut nommer quelques-uns des érudits jaina contemporains cités par M. Alsdorf: en particulier le śvetāmbara Puṇyavijaya, les digambara A.N. Upadhye, H.L. Jain. Louis Renou a plusieurs fois rendu compte, dans ce journal, des excellents et nombreux travaux publiés par ces deux derniers et sous leur direction (cf. 249, 1961, p. 88 et suiv.; 251, 1963, p. 286; etc.). Grâce aux *Études jaina*, le lecteur peut prendre connaissance de l'impulsion qu'ils ont donnée aux recherches, et de leurs brillants succès. Ils sont les coéditeurs de deux collections passablement fournies, la Jīvarāja Jaina Granthamālā (Sholapur), et la Mūrtidevī Jaina Granthamālā (Bhāratīya Jnānapīṭha Prakāśana, Delhi-Bénarès): à ce jour, dix-huit textes ont été édités dans la première, trente-trois dans la seconde. Au reste, les indianistes n'ignorent pas que A.N. Upadhye a plusieurs fois collaboré à la Singhī Jaina Granthamālā (Bhāratīya Vidyā Bhavan, Bombay). L'immensité de l'oeuvre accomplie par le Muni Puṇyavijayajī, homme d'action autant qu'érudit et religieux vénéré, mérite l'admiration reconnaissante de tous ceux qui s'intéressent à l'Inde. Imagine-t-on la ténacité, la force d'organisation nécessaires pour faire réaménager les bhaṇḍār, regrouper les collections de manuscrits, pour les préserver, convaincre éventuellement leurs propriétaires de s'en séparer (cf. L. Alsdorf, *Neues von alten Jaina-Bibliotheken,* in *Beiträge zur indischen Philologie und Altertumskunde.* Walther Schubring zum 70. Geburtstag dargebracht von der deutschen Indologie)? Dix mille manuscrits de sa propre collection ont constitué le premier fonds du L.D. Institute of Indology construit à Ahmedabad en 1957, grâce à la générosité et à l'intelligence de mécènes jaina, au nombre desquels le célèbre Kasturbhai. On doit d'autre part à Puṇyavijaya de nombreux ouvrages, catalogues de manuscrits (cf. le c.r. de Jean Filliozat, *JA*, 251, 1963, p. 393), éditions importantes; il prépare actuellement l'édition critique du Canon śvetāmbara, à la demande d'une institution jaina de Bombay, le Mahāvīra Jaina Vidyālaya (*The Jaina Āgama Texts Series,* 17 volumes prévus).

La mème institution, qui a publié en 1956 l'*Ācārya Vijayavallabhasūri Commemoration Volume,* vient de livrer le *Golden Jubilee Volume* qui célèbre le cinquantenaire de sa fondation (Bombay, 1968).

A Ahmedabad mème, un groupe de savants travaille en étroite collaboration avec le Muni Puṇyavijayajī. On se bornera à citer un élève du Paṇḍit Sukhlāljī, le Pt. Dalsukh Mālvaṇiyā, directeur du L.D. Institute, lui aussi animateur infatigable. Coéditeur de la Prākrit Text Society (cinq titres à ce jour, dont l'*Aṅgavijjā*, le *Cauppannamahāpurisacariyaṃ*, présentés dans ce journal par Louis Renou, *JA*, 246, 1958, p. 99, et Jean Filliozat, *JA*, 250, 1962, p. 648), il est également responsable de la collection éditée par son Institut (cinq volumes parus). Il espère pouvoir publier prochainement un *Agamic Index : Prakrit Proper Names,* qui sera en quelque sorte la contrepartie du *Dictionary of Pāli Proper Names* de Malalasekera.

Ainsi la Communauté entière fait preuve d'un très grand zèle: hommes d'affaires, érudits, laïcs, religieux, śvetāmbara, digambara, rivalisent d'ardeur pour permettre les progrès des études jaina.

R.N. DANDEKAR

LUDWIG ALSDORF: *Vorderindien. Bharat–Pakistan–Ceylon.* Eine Landes- und Kulturkunde. gr.8°. 336 p. 59 Abb. auf 32

Taf. 21 Karten, 4 Diagramme, Tab. 1 Taf. i. Anh. Georg Westermann Vlg., Braunschweig–Berlin–Hamburg–München–Kiel–Darmstadt (1955). DM 22,–.

A.'s *Vorderindien* can by no means be characterised as a regular history of the Indian sub-continent. Indeed, it is not intended to be one. Its claim is more modest. It attempts to present, within a comparatively small compass and without any pretence of original scholarship, the significant facts about the geography, population, government and economic conditions of modern India, Pakistan and Ceylon. In his foreword, A. speaks—certainly not with any historical precision—of the three regions, namely, Europe (without the Soviet Union), China of the 18 provinces and India, which together cover one tenth of the earth's surface but which is inhabited by one half of the entire human population, as being the seats of the three great living cultures. He then proceeds to give, in about four paragraphs, an outline of the history of India with special reference to her contacts with the worlds of the West and of the East. In this connection, one is inclined to feel that a whole chap., by way of a culture-historical introduction, would have been more apropos. Such a chap. would have helped to set the recent happenings and the present situation in their proper perspective. As it is, the *Einführung* is rather journalistic in character.

Coming to the main part of the book, however, one does not fail to be impressed by the fact that A. has collected his material with great care and discrection. He has always sought to draw, for his information, on the most recent available sources and on the experiences gathered in the course of his several visits to these countries, and has presented his facts and figures in a systematic manner. But what strikes one is that there is very little of what may be called 'interpretation' of those facts and figures. A.'s book, accordingly, tends to become just a sort of a catalogue. Dealing with population e.g., A. has had naturally to refer to caste-system and untouchability. But his treatment of the topic appears to be rather too sketchy. He should have indicated the various factors which had contributed to the evolution and consolidation of this unique social phenomenon, pointed out its strengths and weaknesses, and clearly stated how it actually functioned at the present day. Similarly, in the chap. entitled *Der Mensch,* one expects to read something about the way of life and thought of the people; but one is disappointed. Mere reproduction of census figures and related statistics does not tell much about what an Indian man is like. The section on 'Indian culture and human culture' cannot be said to be adequate. The chs. dealing with political and economic conditions generally reveal a sympathetic understanding of the situation on the part of A. His brief notices of the 21 regions within the sub-continent speak for his essentially practical approach to the subject. The large number of statistical tables, maps and diagrams, which illustrate the text, must be mentioned as a special feature of this book. The photographs also are well chosen.

It must be remembered that generally the 3 countries about which A. has written, and more particularly India, are still going through a process of regeneration. Since the attainment of independence after a long spell of foreign domination, they have been earnestly trying to discover themselves anew. They are seeking, so to say, to find their own 'souls'. New norms and ideals—social, political and economic—are gradually emerging. The Indian National Congress, which, incidentally, still continues to be the most powerful political party in the country, has, e.g., pledged itself to the evolution of a socialistic pattern of society. And its concept of socialism certainly differs in several fundamental respects from the academic concept of socialism. This being so, any statements that may have been made about India — and particularly about her economic life — are soon apt to become out-of-date. Notwithstanding this, the book under review will serve as a useful and sufficiently reliable handbook for a foreigner who takes an intelligent interest in the affairs of the Indian sub-continent.

A.M. GHATAGE

Apabhraṃśa-Studien. von LUDWIG ALSDORF. Leipzig. 1937. Pp. viii + 113. Price RM. 2.50.

The present volume of ALSDORF consists of 12 articles dealing with some problems of the linguistic and metrical aspects of Apabhraṃśa language and literature. Except for the discussion about the formation of the Present Tense, he limits himself to the verses quoted by Hemacandra in his *Prakrit Grammar* and a few additional ones collected by PISCHEL in his *Materialien.*

Two of his articles in the present volume deal with the metrical and textual corrections of PISCHEL, a work which he had begun in one of his articles contributed to the *Festschrift Winternitz.* More interesting are, however, his other articles, dealing with some difficult problems about Ap. morphology. He is unwilling to admit the rule of Hemacandra that in Ap. the mere crude form of the word can be used for the Nom. Acc. and Gen. cases. Some other rules which he has attempted to formulate are: (1) All words in Ap. having more than two syllables shorten their final vowels: (2) If *m* or any other nasal is dropped between two vowels, the second of the two is nasalised and not the first as would be expected: (3) The change of *s* to *h* was an earlier law of the Ap. language, while after some time it stopped to have effect: (4) Vowels followed by other vowels are lengthened and the following vowels are dropped.

More doubtful are his other suggestions like the equation between Ap. *tūra* Gr. *tūros* meaning 'cheese'; his denial that the passive forms are not used in an active sense as interpreted by PISCHEL; (where his suggested idiom of offering oneself as a *bali* seems unnatural to an Indian ear), and his suggestion that at least a few verses from Hemacandra's quotations must have been composed by him, on the reason that no poet would go on using three or four forms of gerund in one and the same verse, (when we remember the inclinations of many Indian authors to compose works after works with such an intention); and his suggestion to postulate two dialects of Ap. according to the sect of the writer, even though we must admit different dialects in Ap. and he is justified in criticising BLOCH, GRAY and others on the score of neglecting this vital point. An exhaustive Ap. grammar, however, showing the different dialectic differences is yet to be written and studies of the present type will be of great use to such an end.

J.C. HEESTERMAN

Ludwig Alsdorf, *Beiträge zur Geschichte von Vegetarismus und*

Rinderverehrung in Indien (=*Akademie der Wissenschaften und der Litteratur in Mainz, Abhn. der Geistes- und Sozialwiss. Klasse,* Jahrg. 1961, Nr. 6). Wiesbaden, in Kommission bei Franz Steiner Verlag GmbH., 1962. 69 pp.

Vegetarianism, or rather *ahiṃsā*, and sanctity of bovine animals (not only the cow, as the author rightly stresses), although never general or even valid for the majority of Hindus, have come to be recognized as the hallmark of Hinduism. Patriots in search of national identity have invoked these doctrines. They can be said to be part of the national ideology of modern India. For all that they put baffling problems to the administrator and the economic planner. An inquiry into origin and cause of the twin doctrines does not only present an academic interest, it has a bearing on India's present day reality as well. It is therefore to be welcomed that Professor Alsdorf compressed his findings in an eminently readable essay, that should appeal also to the non-sanskritist.

In accordance with the title the author's viewpoint is purely historical. The problem he has set himself concerns the historical development of the twin doctrines, not their meaning. (Paraphrases like "magisch-ritualistisches Tabu auf das Leben", p. 15, will not be intended as an explanation). Accordingly the author seeks an answer to the question when and in what form the twin doctrines arose and developed; or rather, when and how they manifested themselves in the texts. The Vedic texts do not know the *ahiṃsā* doctrine and enjoin the killing of cows and bull at certain occasions (e.g. at the ceremonial reception of a guest). It is only in the later *dharma* literature that the *ahiṃsā* doctrine and the inviolability of the cow find full expression. The matter is further complicated by the fact that the *dharma* texts contradictorily contain both the Vedic injunctions and the rigorous demands of *ahiṃsā* and vegetarianism. The historical approach seems to impose itself. In the author's view the contradictions of the texts can mean only one thing: a chronological succession.

The demonstration centres on the relevant part of Manu (V, 5-55), where three successive layers are recogized. The first layer is represented by the discussion on pure and impure food (5-25); there is no question of *ahiṃsā*. This stage is also represented by the *dharmasūtras*. The next stage comes with the verses 27-44, where *ahiṃsā* is the rule, except the case of Vedic injunctions when meat is allowed or even obligatory. The last stage is reached in 44-55, where *ahiṃsā* and vegetarianism are absolute.

The sanctity of the cow — rightly kept separate from *ahiṃsā* — shows a roughly parallel development. The special position of the bovine is abundantly attested in the Vedic texts. This did not preclude the consumption of beef (not much of an argument, however, for an otherwise unassailable case can be derived from the absence of the cow in the old lists of non-consumable meat, p. 59. The criterion is here, as the author has pointed out previously, impurity. One would hardly expect to find the cow among the impure animals). The next stage is found in some of the older *smṛtis,* where eating beef is restricted to sacrificial occasions. This restriction is then, in the later *smṛtis*, subsumed under the one regarding all meat. (Alsdorf's second layer in the development of *ahiṃsā*, above). Thus the sanctity of the cow has become intimately linked with the *ahiṃsā* doctrine.

This clear-cut chronological frame has much to recommendi t-self to the western scholar. I doubt, however, whether it can do justice to the Indian facts, even if we should limit ourselves to the texts. The limitations of the chronological perspective stand out clearly when the author, in his search for historical origins, is forced back away from the texts into the limbo of pre-Aryan civilization and the ruins of Harappa. Although the hypothesis of pre-Aryan origins of Hindu ideas and institutions is far from impossible, this reasoning also means that, because of lack of documentation, the problem is shifted out of sight and rendered all but meaningless. The author further surmises—quite consistently—that not only *ahiṃsā* and sanctity of the bovine, but also their opposite, (ritual) bloodshed, finds its roots in pre-Aryan civilization. Indeed, as the author observes, the juxtaposition of these opposites in pre-Aryan times is no more illogical than their existence side by side in Hinduism till the present day.

Even if, some cases, we can feel confident that "kritisch-historischer Betrachtung löst sich also das scheinbare Nebeneinander widersprechender Vorschriften auf in das Nacheinander geschichtlicher Entwicklungsstufen" (p. 17), we must nevertheless admit "das so typisch indische Nebeneinander nach unserem Empfinden unvereinbarer Gegensätze" (p. 42 n. 1; cf. p. 54). One wonders, however, how, in the Indian view, these opposites are reconciled. Are we forced to consider Indian culture as a meaningless jumble? Here a different line of inquiry can no longer be avoided. Having exhausted the historical question we are faced with the problem of meaning. Here only the beginning of an answer can be indicated. One could start with the apparent persistence of the two opposites. It would seem that, far from presenting an inconsistency, there is a link between them. The link can be illustrated by one of the author's own observations, namely that the monk (who does not kill) can lead a sinless life thanks to the sin of the layman (who does the killing for him).

Going further along this line we note that a similar situation seems to obtain in the Vedic ritual: the sacrificer has to abstain, among other things, from meat; the *ṛtvij* on the other hand is obliged to consume the meat. The sacrificer eats afterwards. The *ṛtvij* who would refuse to eat the sacrificial meat is threatened by Manu with dire consequences. It has been pointed out by Thieme that the basic pattern of the Vedic sacrifice is that of a banquet offered to both divine and human guests. Now the ceremonial reception of the guest (the sacrificial priest is expressly mentioned as such) involves the offering of a cow to the guest. The guest has to give the order for the killing (or he may order to set the animal free), that is, he takes the onus of the killing upon himself, thus enabling the host to partake of the meat. This is probably the reason why Buddhist and Jain monks, though practising *ahiṃsā*, originally could accept meat, on the condition that it was not expressly prepared for them (cf. p. 5 ff.).

The ritual texts show a marked aversion to killing. Nevertheless the sacrifice is essential to the maintenance of life. Time and again life has to be rewon out of death. Therefore one party (*ṛtvij*, guest) has to take upon himself the onus of death so that the other may win life. Thus the sacrifice involves the participants in the ever recurring alternation of life and death.

The decisive point in the development is the breakthrough, out of the vicious life-death circle, that is, the rise of the renunciatory way of life, where death is no longer periodically conquered, but permanently eliminated. It would seem that it is in this direction that we have to look for the meaning of *ahiṃsā*, the avoidance of death, death being otherwise inextricably connected with life. *Ahiṃsā* therefore is proper to the renouncer of the world, its opposite belongs to the sphere of the man-in-the-world. The interaction, as L. Dumont has pointed out, between these two spheres (in Indian terms *nivṛtti* and *pravṛtti*) seems to be central to Hinduism (past as well as present) (cf. L. Dumont, "Le renoncement dans les religions de l'Inde", *Arch. de Soc. des Rel.*, no. 7 (1959)). If I am right this may explain the persistent juxtaposition of the irreconcilable opposites. At the same time it would seem that the search for meaning may deliver a clue to the problem of origin as well.

These few and necessarily sketchy reflections cannot possibly do justice to the author's many interesting and detailed observations (e.g. on the supposed Buddhist and Jain origins of *ahiṃsā*; Buddhism and Jainism are shown, together with brahmanism, to participate in a common movement). The reviewer's reflections are meant as a tribute to the stimulating quality of this interesting study. Professor Alsdorf has given us a most welcome contribution to our knowledge of Indian religious concepts and practices.

OSKAR VON HINÜBER

A Critical Pāli Dictionary begun by V. Trenckner. Vol. II. Editor-in-Chief: L. Alsdorf. Fascicule 6 (1970), 7 (1971), 8 (1973), 9 (1975), 10 (1979). Copenhagen

In dem seit dem Erscheinen des ersten Teiles dieser „Bemerkungen" (KZ 84, 1970, 177-186) verstrichenen Jahrzehnt sind die Faszikel II. 6-10 (1970-1979) des Critical Pāli Dictionary erschienen, die die Stichwörter *āha* bis *uparima* enthalten. Ihre endgültige Gestalt verdanken sie in nicht wenigen Fällen vor allem dem unermüdlichen Wirken von L. Alsdorf, der seit dem Faszikel II. 5 als „editor-in-chief" das CPD leitete, und der in seinem letzten Lebensjahrzehnt dem Wörterbuch den weitaus größten Teil seiner Arbeitskraft widmete. Daher hat sein unerwarteter Tod eine schwer zu schließende und schmerzlich empfundene Lücke vor allem auf dem Gebiet der Pāli-Lexikographie hinterlassen. Unter seiner straffen Führung, die nicht selten, besonders aber in II. 9 und II. 10 eine weitgehende Neugestaltung und Umformung des Materials mit sich brachte, konnte das Wörterbuch wenigstens in seiner äußeren Form zu einer weitgehenden Einheitlichkeit zurückgeführt und das Material, dessen Flut das Lexikon oft zu ertränken drohte, eingedämmt werden. Trotz dieser Bemühungen konnte jedoch die hohe Qualität des ersten Bandes nicht wieder erreicht werden.

Nachdem die Faszikel II. 6-10 bereits mehrfach in meist recht allgemein gehaltenen Besprechungen vorgestellt worden sind[1]) — eine Ausnahme bilden nur die wichtigen, auch in Einzelheiten gehenden Rezensionen von C. Caillat und K.R. Norman —, sollen hier nach einer kurzen Vorbemerkung Berichtigungen und Ergänzungen zu den einzelnen Artikeln zusammengestellt werden.

Vor allem in den letzten Faszikeln hat der Artikelaufbau einige, wohl nicht immer glückliche Änderungen gegenüber dem ersten Band erfahren. Um das Material zu straffen, werden nun nicht nur alle Personen mit demselben Namen unter einem Lemma zusammengefaßt (seit II. 10: *Upatissa, Upananda*), sondern auch alle Komposita unter dem Vorderglied aufgeführt, was eine Störung der alphabetischen Reihenfolge nach sich zieht (*uttari, upakkama*). Einschneidender ist der seit II. 7 vom wohldurchdachten Vorbild des ersten Bandes abweichende Aufbau der Verb-Artikel. Im Artikelkopf erscheint nun ein Formenkatalog ohne Belegstellen. Da zugleich im Artikel selbst keine Bestimmung der einzelnen Formen mehr vorgenommen wird, bleibt der Benutzer im Zweifel, ob etwa die mehrdeutige Form *uggahesi*, Vin IV 161, 20 als Praesens oder als Aorist angesehen wird, da das CPD neben *uggaṇhāti* irrtümlich auch *uggaheti* (s. u.) ansetzt.

Auch die mangelhafte Abstimmung mit dem ersten Band wird

1. Über die KZ 84, 1970, 178 Anm. 1 angeführten Besprechungen hinaus sind mir die folgenden Rezensionen und Anzeigen bekannt geworden: II.1: E. Frauwallner, WZKSO 5, 1961, 169f.; II. 2: E. Frauwallner, WZKSO 7, 1963, 211f.; II.3-5: E. Frauwallner, WZKSO 14, 1970, 210; II.4: C. Caillat, IF 74, 1969, 223-225; II.4-5: T. Rajapatirana, IIJ 14, 1972, 102f.; II.5: C. Caillat, IF 75, 1970, 299-303; II.6: C. Caillat, IF 79, 1974, 250-252; L.A. Schwarzschild, JAOS 93, 1973, 376f.; P. Horsch, OLZ 1974, 493f.; II. 6-8: J.-Ch. Coppieters, JAs 1976, 480f.; II.7: C. Caillat: IF 78, 1973, 247-249; L.A. Schwarzschild, JAOS 95, 1975, 153f.; II.7-8: K.R. Norman: OLZ 1979, 391-394; II. 8: C. Caillat, IF 79, 1974, 252-255; L.A. Schwarzschild, JAOS 96, 1976, 360f.; T. Rajapatirana. IIJ 18, 1976, 140; P.V. Bapat, ABORI 56, 1976, 250; II.9: C. Caillat. IF 81, 1976, 327-329; K.R. Norman, JRAS 1977, 127f. und OLZ 1979, 493-495; L.G. Schwarzschild. JAOS 99, 1979, 517.—Außerdem hat L. Alsdorf regelmäßig über das Fortschreiten des CPD im Jahrbuch der Mainzer Akademie berichtet.

beim Benutzer gelegentlich Verwirrung stiften (s.u. *uddhacchidda-vātapāna; upagamma/anupagamma*), wenn s. v. *issuka,* ifc. zwar die Meinung von CPD I zurückgewiesen wird, daß es sich um einen Überlieferungsfehler für *(an)ussuka* handele, ohne daß das CPD II sich damit auseinandersetzt, daß in CPDI I für *(an) ussuka* und *(an)issukin* ganz verschiedene Bedeutungen angesetzt sind.

Nicht nur mit Verweisen zum ersten Band, auch mit Querverweisen innerhalb des zweiten wird gegeizt (*ukkara/ukkura*; *udaka-niddhamanatumba/udakatumba* etc.). Auf der anderen Seite führen Kettenverweise in die Irre: von *ukkaṇṭhita* zu *ukkaṇṭhanā* zu *ukkaṇṭhati,* wo sich zwei weit auseinander liegende Bedeutungen finden, deren Verteilung auf die beiden anderen Stichwörter im Dunkel bleibt.

Schwerer wiegen die immer wieder im sprachgeschichtlichen Teil der Artikel zutage tretenden Mängel, die oft mit philologischen Mitteln behoben werden können. Um dem Anspruch, ein „Critical" Pāli Dictionary zu sein, zu genügen, sollte es jedem Mitarbeiter selbstverständlich sein, einen Blick wenigstens in den kritischen Apparat der bis auf wenige Ausnahmen oft herzlich schlecht edierten europäischen Ausgaben zu werfen[2]). In einigen Fällen hätte dies weit in die Irre gehende sprachliche Beurteilungen vermieden (s.u. *udrabhati*) oder zur Heilung von Abschnitten, die im CPD als unheilbar verderbt angesehen werden, geführt (s. u. *udājita*). Deshalb sei nachdrücklich an den letzten Abschnitt der Einleitung (CPD I. S. X) erinnert, der es als Hauptanliegen des Wörterbuchs bezeichnet, Schwächen der europäischen Textausgaben zu beheben.

Daß man sich bei der Bestimmung der Etymologie eine häufigere Verwendung von R.L. Turner: A Comparative Dictionary of the Indo-Aryan Languages. London 1966 (CDIAL) wünschte, sei nur am Rande erwähnt (etwa CDIAL Nr. 1710 *utkara* zu *ukkāra*).

Diese, wenigstens zum Teil nur Äußerlichkeiten betreffenden Mängel werfen kaum einen Schatten auf die Tatsache, daß die

2. Einen spürbaren Fortschritt bringen die Neuausgaben von Thūp: The Chronicle of the Thūpa and the Thūpavaṃsa by N.A. Jayawickrama. London 1971 und von demselben Autor: Vimānavatthu and Petavatthu. London 1977. Leider hat Jayawickrama hier eine neue Verszählung eingeführt, die von der des CPD unregelmäßig abweicht.

Kenntnis des Pāli mit dem Voranschreiten des CPD erheblich gefördert wird. Auch wo die oft naheliegende Lösung eines Problems verfehlt wird, erleichtert das ausgebreitete Material eine Richtigstellung. Und in zahlreichen Fällen werden vom CPD selbst Schwierigkeiten ausgeräumt. In diesem Zusammenhang sind, um nur einiges zu nennen, die Artikel *isi* oder *iñjati/iñjeti* hervorzuheben, in denen ohne jede Weitschweifigkeit eine klare und wohldokumentierte Darstellung von Gebrauch und Bedeutung der Wörter gegeben wird. Mustergültig ist vor allem die Beschreibung der bezeugten Formen, die in CPD II oft Gefahr läuft, vernachlässigt zu werden, die jedoch eine notwendige Ergänzung zu den nicht immer fehlerfreien Angaben bei W. Geiger: Pāli. Literatur und Sprache. Straßburg 1916, bildet. Unter *isipatana* wird das Problem der Herleitung dieser und verwandter Formen aus dem buddhistischen Sanskrit überzeugend gelöst, und *uttarapāsaka* überholt, ohne ihn zu nennen, A.K. Coomaraswamy, JAOS 48, 1928, 256.

Unbemerkt vom CPD selbst bestätigt das Pāli mitunter die Lehren der altindischen Grammatiker: *āharahattha(ka)* ist ein sonst nur aus Pāṇini 2.1.72 bekannter Kompositionstyp (Ai. Gr. II. 1, S. 316 & 120b); *uttarāmukha* ist nach Pāṇini 5.3.38 gebildet und *uttarāhaka* (s. u. *uttarapāthaka*) wird durch Patañjalis Mahābhāṣya bestätigt.

J.W. DE JONG

Ludwig Alsdorf, *Les études jaina, État présent et tâches futures.* Paris, Collège de France, 1965. iv+96 pp. 10 N.F.

Ludwig Alsdorf, *Die Āryā-Strophen des Pāli-Kanons metrisch hergestellt und textgeschichtlich untersucht* (=*Akademie der Wissenschaften und der Literatur, Abh. d. Geistes- u. sozialw. Kl.*, Jahrgang 1967, Nr. 4). 89 pp. DM 14,—.

Les conférences, faites par M. Ludwig Alsdorf au printemps 1965 au Collège de France, sont d'un très grand intérêt, non seulement pour le cercle restreint des specialistes du jainisme qui lisent le francais mais aussi pour tous les indianistes. En particulier, les spécialistes du bouddhisme ont beaucoup à apprendre de cet exposé lucide où il est souvent question de problèmes de la philologie bouddhique. M. Alsdorf commence par souligner l'importance de la comparaison du bouddhisme et du jainisme, deux religions nées dans les mêmes conditions et à la même époque. Il montre à l'aide de quelques exemples —*phasu*(*ya*), *āsava*, *māla-vihāra*, *tāī*—que la même terminologie se retrouve dans les textes jainas et bouddhiques. Après avoir brièvement caractérisé la littérature jaina et sa contribution à la religion, la philosophie et la littérature de l'Inde, M. Alsdorf esquisse son importance pour l'étude du prākrit, de l'apabhraṃśa et des langues dravidiennes. Ensuite il examine le problème que pose la langue des textes anciens du canon et la possibilité de déceler les traces d'une langue pré-canonique, la 'véritable' ardhamāgadhī qui se caractérise par l'*s* occidental comme seule sifflante, *l* oriental pour *r* et *-e* au lieu de *-o* à partir de *-as*. Selon lui, la traduction ou l'adaptation linguistique des textes jainas en prākrit canonique a dû avoir lieu longtemps avant le concile de Valabhī au cinquième siècle, probablement à l'époque même où le canon bouddhique primitif était traduit en pāli. Le parallélisme avec les travaux de Lüders sur la langue du canon bouddhique primitif est évident. Comme Lüders, M. Alsdorf fait appel au témoignage des inscriptions d'Aśoka pour déterminer les caractéristiques des dialectes occidental et oriental. De même que Lüders avait découvert un abl. sing. en *-am* en pāli, M. Alsdorf en démontre l'existence dans un texte canonique jaina: *Uttarādhyayana* 23,46.[1] Espérons que M. Alsdorf entreprendra lui-même d'écrire "Les considérations sur la langue du canon jaina primitif" qu'il considère comme une des tâches les plus importantes des études jaina.

En passant ensuite en revue les éditions des textes canoniques jainas dont on dispose à présent M. Alsdorf constate que, pour 21 des 48 textes canoniques, il existe des éditions de style européen mais que la plupart devraient être refaites. M. Alsdorf attire l'attention sur les éditions du canon publiées par les Sthānakvāsin, une secte réformatrice du début du dix-huitième siècle, et l'intérêt que présente le nombre et l'ordre des textes dans ces éditions. Il

1. M. John Brough fait remarquer que l'on peut aussi expliquer des formes pālies en *-aṃ* comme dues à une erreur graphique, le scribe ayant écrit *-aṃ* au lieu de *-ā* (*The Gāndhārī Dharmapada*, London, 1962, pp. 79-80). M. Alsdorf ne discute pas cette possibilité et s'appuie sur la tradition pour maintenir la forme *visabhakkhaṇaṃ* (*Uttarādhyayana* 23, 46). Pourtant il n'hésite pas pur correger ailleurs le texte de l'*Uttarādhyayana* à l'encontre de la tradition (cf. p. 41 où, dans *Utt.* 25, 7, il propose de lire *janna-jaṭṭhā* au lieu de *jannaṭṭhā*).

examine ensuite la valeur des commentaires en prākrit (*niryukti* et *cūrṇi*)et en sanskrit (*ṭīkā*) pour l'établissement d'éditions critiques. M. Alsdorf montre que des fautes métriques et des fausses sanskritisations témoignent du fait que, malgré une tradition orale et écrite ininterrompue, les textes canoniques n'ont pas été préservés de la déformation et de la corruption.[2] Selon lui, il faudrait manifester encore plus d'indépendance à leur égard quel'on a fait jusqu'à présent.

M. Alsdorf s'étend plus en détail sur l'importance de la métrique pour l'étude de la chronologie du canon jaina. C'est surtout l'*āryā* qui permet de déterminer l'âge relatif d'un texte ou d'un passage d'un texte: "les textes en āryā sont ipso facto récents, des āryās à l'intérieur de textes en mètres anciens, ou bien en vieille prose, sont des adjonctions plus récentes ou des citations". M. Alsdorf décrit la forme classique de l'*āryā* ainsi qu'une forme archaïque qui ne se rencontre que dans trois chapitres des textes canoniques et une variante semi- prosaïque, le *veḍha*. Avant d'étudier l'*āryā* dans le canon jaina et, en particulier, dans l'*Uttarādhyayana*, M. Alsdorf examine l'emploi de l'*āryā* dans les textes pālis. L'*āryā* archaïque s'y rencontre surtout dans le *Suttanipāta* où elle avait été signalée déjà par Jacobi en 1895 (*Jaina Sutras,* Part 2, SBE, 45, p. 271, n. 2) et dans quelques autres textes. L'*āryā* classique se trouve dans six *jātaka* (Nos. 542, 525, 485, 479, 358 et 301). En étudiant ces *jātaka* M. Alsdorf montre que leur contenu confirme leur caractère récent par rapport à des *jātaka* dont les vers sont en *śloka* ou en *triṣṭubh*. Cette conclusion est corroborée par l'examen des *āryā* dans les *jātaka* du *Mahāvastu* et dans les *Therīgāthā*. Après les *jātaka et les Therīgāthā* c'est le début du *Mahāvagga* qui contient le plus grand nombre d'*āryā*. M. Alsdorf constate que "l'utilisation relativement fréquente et visiblement originale de l'āryā éloigne considérablement ce texte dans le temps du deuxième fragment ancien de biographie de Bouddha, le Mahaparinibbāna-

2. A propos du pāli *bhūnaha* ou *bhūnahu* M. Alsdorf remarque que Baburam Saksena a indiqué la bonne étymologie en 1936 (*BSOS*, VIII, p. 713). Déjà H. Kern avait proposé la même étymologie, cf. *Bijdrage tot de verklaring van eenige woorden in Pali-geschriften voorkomende* (Amsterdam, 1886), pp. 52-53; *Toevoegselen op 't woordenboek van Childers*, I (Amsterdam, 1916), pp. 5-6. Kern avait aussi déjà proposé de lire *muñcantu* au lieu de *pamuñcantu* dans *Jātaka* III, p. 179 (*Bijdrage, p.* 79; cf. L. Alsdorf, *Die Āryā-Strophen des Pāli-Kanons*, p. 24).

sutta". Quelques *āryā* se trouvent encore dans les *Theragāthā*, le *Sagāthavagga*, le *Vimānavatthu*, le *Petavatthu* et l'*Apadāna*. Le nombre total des *āryā* archaïques s'élève à 46, celui des *āryā* classiques à environ 450. Alors que chez les jainas l'*āryā* prédomine dans la littérature postcanonique, le mètre normal de la littérature postcanonique en pāli est le *śloka*. M. Alsdorf constate deux exceptions: le *Nettipakaraṇa* et le *Petakopadesa* et les préfaces et les épilogues des commentaires de Buddhaghosa. Selon M. Alsdorf, ces exceptions s'expliquent par le fait que l'émigration du pāli au Ceylan a arrêté l'emploi de l'*āryā* dans la littérature pālie. Le *Nettipakaraṇa* a dû être écrit par un indien du nord de l'Inde dont Buddhaghosa est aussi originaire. Le *Peṭakopadesa* est une suite du *Nettipakaraṇa* et son auteur l'a pillé largement.

Aprés avoir étudié l'*āryā* dans la littérature pālie M. Alsdorf revient au canon jaina. Il démontre que l'*Uttarādhyayana* contient environ 129 *āryā* dont 109 se trouvent dans six chapitres du dernier tiers du texte. Plusieurs passages, écrits dans ce mètre, contiennent des développements scholastiques et dogmatiques d'origine plus récente. En outre, 45 de ces 109 *āryā* se retrouvent dans des textes canoniques récents. D'un intérêt particulier est un passage, rédigé en *āryā*, relatif au goût, à l'odeur et au toucher des *leśyā*. Ce passage témoigne d'une élaboration scholastique de la théorie karmanique des *leśyā* "couleurs de l'âme".

Dans la derniére partie de ce petit livre l'auteur mentionne comme une des tâches futures des études jaina la reprise du travail sur l'*Āvaśyaka* par Ernst Leumann et, en premier lieu, une édition critique de l'*Āvaśyakaniryukti*. Pour terminer M. Alsdorf attire l'attention sur la littérature des *digambara* et, en particulier, sur les problèmes que suscite la publication récente de textes anciens, le *Ṣaṭkhaṇḍāgama* et le *Kaṣāyaprābhṛta* avec les commentaires qui s'y rattachent. M. Alsdorf montre que ces textes contiennent des passages qui se retrouvent dans des textes des *śvetāmbara*. Le phénomène s'observe en plus grande mesure dans d'autres textes des *śvetāmbara*: le *Mūlācāra* de Vaṭṭakera et la *Mūlāradhanā* de Śivārya.

J'espére avoir réussi à montrer l'intérêt que présente l'ouvrage de M. Alsdorf pour tous ceux qui s'intéressent de loin ou de près aux études jaina. Espérons que de jeunes indianistes seront inspirés par les perspectives tracées, de manière magistrale, par l'auteur. Il constate avec regret une certaine récession des études jaina dans l'indologie du présent. Peut-être ce phénomène s'explique par le fait que les études jaina sont d'un accés assez difficile et se sont développées dans un certain isolement. M. Alsdorf montre bien que les difficultés ne sont pas insurmontables et que l'isolement doit être rompu dans l'intérêt aussi bien des études jaina mêmes, que d'autres branches de l'indianisme et surtout des études bouddhiques.

Sur un seul point l'argumentation de M. Alsdorf ne me paraît pas tout à fait convaincante. Il est hors de doute que l'*āryā* est un indice qui permet de dater un texte par rapport à d'autres textes. M. Alsdorf effectue le passage d'une chronologie à une chronologie absolue en adoptant comme *terminus ante quem* le milieu ou la deuxième moitié du troisième siècle avant J.-Chr.: "la suite de l'évolution de l'*āryā* en pāli est évidemment arrêtée par son émigration vers Ceylan, qui date du milieu ou de la deuxième moitié du IIIe siècle avant J.-Chr. Tout ce qu'il y a en fait d'āryās dans le canon pāli doit être plus ancien" (p. 70). C'est le même *terminus ante quem* que M. Alsdorf propose pour la traduction du canon bouddhique primitif en pāli: "Pour cette dernière le sûr *terminus ante quem* est l'introduction de textes pālis au Ceylan, c'est-à-dire selon l'opinion courante au milieu du IIIe siècle avant J.-Chr." Je ne sais pas si c'est l'opinion courante mais, en tout cas, cette opinion doit se baser surtout sur la tradition singhalaise selon laquelle Mahinda, le fils d'Asoka, a introduit à Ceylan le canon pāli. M. Ét. Lamotte a bien montré l'invraisemblance de cette tradition (*Histoire du Bouddhisme Indien*, I, Louvain, 1958, p. 339). Un autre problème qui se pose est le suivant. Est-ce-que des passages plus récents, rédigés en *āryā*, se sont déjà adjoints au canon primitif ou est-ce qu'ils se sont produits seulement après sa transposition en pāli? En ce qui concerne l'*āryā* archaïque la conclusion de M. Alsdorf est la suivante: "Que l'āryā ancienne n'apparaît nettement que dans des textes anciens du canon pāli, que la plupart des exemples se rencontrent dans un texte comme le Suttanipāta — cela correspond tout à fait au rôle qu'elle joue dans le canon jaina." Il y a dans le canon pāli aussi de nombreuses *āryā* qu'il faut considérer comme des formes de transition entre l'*āryā* archaïque et l'*āryā* classique (cf. p. 68). Malheureusement, M. Alsdorf ne donne pas un inventaire des passages qui contiennent de telles *āryā*. Ces formes de transition qui semblent être bien plus rares chez les jainas compliquent les problèmes chronologiques. Je ne peux que signaler ici ces problèmes qui méritent d'être étudiés plus en détail.

Dans *Die Āryā-Strophen des Pāli-Kanons metrisch hergestellt und textgeschichtlich untersucht* M. Alsdorf établit un texte correct du point de vue métrique pour toutes les *āryā* du canon pāli à l'exception de celles qui se trouvent dans les *Thera-* et *Therīgāthā.*[3] La première partie donne les textes en *āryā* archaïques. En ce qui concerne la louange du Buddha par Upāli (*MN* I 386,3-32) on s'étonne que l'auteur ne fasse pas mention du fragment de la recension sanskrite publiée par Hoernle (*Manuscript Remains,* pp. 27-35). La publication de Hoernle contient aussi une étude de la version chinoise par Watanabe. Ce dernier travil n'est pas exempt d'erreurs et il y aurait lieu d'étudier de nouveau les différentes recensions de ce texte en tenant compte des corrections que M. Alsdorf propose pour le texte pāli.

Parmi les textes en *āryā* classique le plus intéressant est sans doute le début du *Mahāvagga* dans lequel M. Alsdorf a retrouvé dix-neuf strophes écrites dans ce mètre.[4] M. Alsdorf ne se contente

3. Cf. *The Thera- and Therī-Gāthā,* ed. H. Oldenberg and R. Pischel. Second edition with Appendices by K.R. Norman and L. Alsdorf (London, Pali Text Society, 1966), pp. 233-250.

4. Selon M. Alsdorf le grand nombre de strophes *āryā* dans ce texte n'a pas été pris en considération jusqu'à maintenant. Toutefois il faut faire remarquer que ces strophes ont retenu l'attention de plusieurs savants. Déjà Jacobi avait reconnu que la célèbre strophe *ye dhammā hetuppabhavā...*(*Vin.* I, p. 40) était une *āryā* (*ZDMG*, 38, 1884, p. 602). M. Alsdorf rejette les corrections proposées par Jacobi (cf. p. 66) comme l'avait fait avant lui Helmer Smith dans un travail que M. Alsdorf ne mentionne pas (*Analecta Rhytmica, Studia Orientalia* XIX:7, Helsinki, 1954, p. 13). Remarquons en passant que Jacobi est le premier à avoir trouvé des strophes en *āryā* dans le *Suttanipāta* (*Jaina Sutras, SBE,* vol. 45, Oxford, 1895, p. 271, n. 2). En ce qui concerne les neuf strophes qui décrivent la victoire du Buddha sur le *nāga* (*Vin.* I, p. 25, 18-34) Oldenberg a bien reconnu que ce passage est écrit en vers, bien qu'il n'ait pas pu en déterminer le mètre (cf. le passage de "Zur Geschichte der indischen Prosa" cité par M. Alsdorf, pp. 56-57; plus loin M. Alsdolf dit: "Nur weil er die Verse nicht als solche erkannte, konnte Oldenberg..."!). Deux autres strophes en *āryā* (*Vin.* I, p. 40, 24-25 et 33-34; cf. Alsdorf, pp. 64-71) ont été signalées par E.J. Thomas (*The Life of Buddha,* London, 1927, p. 94, n. 1). C'est surtout Helmer Smith qui, à plusiers reprises, a étudié les strophes en *āryā* du *Mahāvagga* (*Saddanīti,* vol. IV, Lund, 1949, pp. 1161-1165; *Les deux prosodies du vers bouddhique,* Lund, 1950, pp. 38-40; *Analecta Rhytmica,* Helsinki, 1954, pp. 13-15). M. Alsdorf ne cite que le deuxième de ces trois travaux.

pas de rétablir un texte correct pour ces strophes mais il discute aussi en détail les problèmes qui résultent de la comparaison avec des textes parallèles en sanskrit et, avant tout, avec le *Catuṣpariṣatsūtra* (*CPS*). Il nous avertit que la relation de la version pālie avec les autres versions (M. Alsdorf parle de versions plus tardives) et, en premier lieu, le *CPS* ne peut être définitivement déterminée qu'après une comparaison détaillée dex textes entiers. Toutefois, il lui semble vraisemblable que la version pālie est la plus ancienne qui soit conservée et aussi la source la plus importante des autres versions. Que la version pālie soit plus authentique que celle, représentée par le *CPS*, n'a pas de quoi nous surprendre, car celui-ci appartient au *Vinaya* des Mūlasarvāstivādin qui est "clos à une époque tardive" (Lamotte, *op. cit.*, p. 187). Il est regrettable que M. Alsdorf n'ait pas consulté les textes parallèles, traduits du chinois, par Ebbe Tuneld (*Recherches sur la valeur des traditions bouddhiques pālie et non-pālie*, Lund, 1915), M. André Migot, ("Un grand disciple du Buddha, Śāriputra", *BEFEO*, XLVI, 1954, pp. 405-554) et M. André Bareau (*Recherches sur la biographie du Buddha dans les Sūtrapiṭaka et les Vinayapiṭaka anciens*, Paris, 1963). Surtout ce dernier travail est de la plus haute importance pour l'étude du début du *Mahāvagga* car M. Bareau a traduit les passages parallèles des *Vinaya* des Mahīśāsaka et des Dharmaguptaka, Vinaya plus anciens que celui des Mūlasarvāstivādin.

Pour terminer qu'il me soit permis d'ajouter quelques remarques de détail à propos du *Mahāvagga*. M. Alsdorf constate que la phrase *anupahacca* ... (*Vin.* I, pp. 24-25) est empruntée au *Pāyāsisuttanta* (corriger en D II 326.2 326 en 336). Il signale aussi que A.P. Buddhadatta corrigé la traduction fautive de ce passage par Rhys Davids. Déjà Leumann avait bien interprété ce passage ("Beziehungen der Jaina-Literatur zu anderen Literaturkreisen", *Actes du sixième congrès international des orientalistes tenu en* 1883 *à Leide*, III, 2, Leide, 1885, p. 479) comme, après lui, Neumann (*Die Reden Gotamo Buddhos*, II, Zürich-Wien, 1957, pp. 760-761) et le *Critical Pāli Dictionary* (p. 198b).

La strophe *appaṃ va bahuṃ* ... (*Vin.* I, p. 40, 24-25) se retrouve

---

Dans une note (p. 52, n. 2), il déclare que, à bien des égards, il ne partage pas les idées de Helmer Smith sur la métrique pālie et moyen-indienne. Espérons que M. Alsdorf trouvera l'occasion de les soumettre à un examen systématique.

dans le *Mahāvastu* III, p. 60, 20-21) et le *CPS* (ed. E. Waldschmidt, p. 378). Dans ce dernier le texte sanskrit est très fragmentaire. D'après la traduction tibétaine, le premier pāda est rétabli par M. Waldschmidt comme *mahyam eva arthena kāryam*. M. Alsdorf remarque: "Das Tibetische hat in der Tat *kho bo la ni don dgos kyi*, aber allein sinnvoll wäre doch *mayham arthenaiva kāryam*! Irrtum oder Nachlässigkeit des tibetischen Übersetzers?" Remarquons que le tibétain ne traduit pas *eva* et que l'ordre des mots en tibétain n'est pas nécessairement le même qu'en sanskrit. C'est pourquoi je propose de rétablir: *arthena mahyam kāryam* (cf. *Mahāvastu: arthena mahyaṃ kāriyaṃ*). Les trois autres pāda du *CPS* correspondent étroitement au texte pāli mais dans un ordre différent (les pāda a, b et d du pāli correspondent aux pāda c, d et b du *CPS*). On ne peut donc pas dire que la strophe du *CPS* correspond à la strophe du *Mahāvastu* où les pāda c et d sont tout à fait différents (cf. Alsdorf, p. 66).

Dans une strophe qui se retrouve deux fois dans le *CPS* M. Waldschmidt a rétabli *a(mara)m* (cf. Alsdorf, p. 67; *CPS*, pp. 380 et 384). Cette reconstruction ne repose pas sur la traduction tibétaine qui a *rjes-su rtogs* (*anugatam*?).

Dans deux strophes, corrigées par M. Alsdorf, il garde la forme *anupatte* à l'encontre de la tradition orientale et de la traduction tibétaine (*Vin*. I, p. 42, 33-37; Alsdorf, p. 69, n. 2; p. 70, n. 2). M. Alsdorf traduit ces deux strophes de la manière suivante: "Als die beiden im Veḷuvana *angekommen* waren ... da prophezeite der Meister von ihnen: 'Hier *kommen* zwei Gefährten'". J'ai mis en italique les mots "angekommen" et "kommen" pour faire ressortir que la leçon *appatte* doit être préférée. Dans la traduction de la version tibétaine il vaudra mieux traduire *'gyur* par le futur: "Ces deux-là seront la meilleure paire de mes Auditeurs" (Alsdorf p. 70: "sind diese beiden das beste Paar meiner Hörer").

C. Krause

Alsdorf Ludwig: *Der Kumārapālapratibodha* Ein Beitrag zur Kenntnis des Apabhraṃśa und der Erzählungs-Literatur der Jainas. Hamburg: Friederichsen, de Gruyter & Co. 1928. (XII, 227 S.) 4° = Alt- und Neu-Indische Studien, hrsg. vom Seminar für Kultur und Geschichte Indiens an der Hamburgischen Universität. RM 12—. Bespr. von Charlotte Krause, Shivpuri/ Indien.

Der Kumārapālapratibodha ist ein umfangreiches Werk der Erzählungs-Literatur der Jainas von der Hand des bekannten Ācārya Sómaprabha Sūri, der es nach eigener Angabe im Jahre 1185 zum Abschluß brachte. Es enthält eine Reihe von Erzählungen, die dogmatische, didaktische, legendäre und andere Themata zum Gegenstand haben und durch die Rahmen-Erzählung von der Bekehrung des Königs Kumārapāla von Gujarat zur Jaina-Religion durch den Ācārya Hemacandra zusammengehalten werden. Der Form nach ist das Werk ein Gemisch von Prosa und Versen. Sein größerer Teil (ca. 40 Erzählungen) ist in Jaina-Mahārāṣṭrī, 5 Erzählungen in Sanskrit, und 2 Erzählungen sowie 3 kleinere eingelegte Stücke und eine Reihe von Einzelversen (insgesamt ca. 250 Strophen) in Apabhraṃśa abgefaßt.

Das Werk ist 1920 als Nr. XIV von Gaekwad's Oriental Series von Muni Jinavijaya herausgegeben worden. Da nach Angabe des Verfassers der vorliegenden Arbeit die Handschrift verloren gegangen ist, geht er von der genannten Ausgabe als Grundlage aus. Sein Ziel ist es, das Apabhraṃśa-Material des Kumārapālapratibodha aufzuschließen.

Der erste, einleitende Teil der Arbeit gibt eine allgemeine Orientierung über den Gegenstand nebst einem alphabetischen Verzeichnis sämtlicher Erzählungen des Werkes, mit Nachweisen von Parallelen.

Der zweite Teil behandelt die Apabhraṃśa-Stücke selbst hinsichtlich ihrer Stoffgeschichte, zu der verschiedenes zu bemerken ist. Die erste, allegorische Apabhraṃśa-Erzählung enhält eine Liste der Kategorien der nicht-erlösten Lebewesen, von der Verfasser p. 17f. feststellt, daß sie von der im Uttarādhyayana- und Jīvājīvābhigama-Sūtra — und wir können hinzufügen, einer Reihe weiterer Āgama-Werke — gegebenen abweicht, während sie mit der der „Karmatheoretiker" übereinstimme. Hierzu sei in Kürze nur soviel bemerkt, daß diese Liste ganz allgemein in den verschiedenen kanonischen und nichtkanonischen Jaina-Schriften ganz verschiedene Gestalten hat, je nach dem jeweiligen im Vordergrund bestehenden Prinzip der Einteilung, und daß

Begriffe wie „*tiryag-yoni*", „*trasa*", „*sthāvara*" usw. in ganz verschiedenen Bedeutungen gebraucht werden, so daß die Feuer- und Windwesen bald als „*trasa*", bald als „*sthāvara*", und die Elementarwesen bald als „*tiryag-yoni*", bald als scheinbar außerhalb der Kategorie stehend erscheinen. Das Prinzip, dem Somaprabha Sūri und, wie Verfasser zeigt, auch Hemacandra folgen, stellt die Vulgat-Auffassung dar, die sich in dem größten Teil der Kommentatoren-Literatur wie im Jīvavicāra-Prakaraṇa und anderen zum „Jaina-Katechismus" gerechneten Schriften findet und deren Ursprung sich z. T. bis in das Bhagavati- und das Prajñāpanā-Sūtra verfolgen läßt. Die Voranstellung der Höllenstufe ist durchaus das allgemeine.

Daß diese allegorische Erzählung dem Dichter Siddhapāla in den Mund gelegt wird, berechtigt kaum zu weiteren Schlüssen, als die man aus der Rolle Hemacandras als Erzähler ziehen zu können glaubte (zu p. 19). Weitere Nachrichten über Siddhapāla enthält der Gujarati-Artikel des Muni Puṇyavijaya,, *Ek Aitihāsik Praśasti*" in Purātattva I, I (saṃvat 1978), pp. 113—21.

Zu der zweiten Apabhraṃśa-Erzählung, der Sthūlabhadra-Kathā, sei nachgetragen: „Sthūlabhadra-Guṇamālā", ein Sanskrit-Gedicht des Vācanācārya Sūracandra (Schülers des Vīrakuśala Gani), das in einer Handschrift im Bhandar von Ghanerav (bei Sadre in Marwar) vorliegt.—Zu den Geschicklichkeitsproben (p. 22, Note „Rājā Bhoja") hätte Hemavijayas Kathāratnākara I, Nr. 18 (Katharatnakara, Das Märchenmeer, Eine Sammlung indischer Erzählungen von Hemavijaya, Deutsch von Johannes Hertel, Band I, München, 1920, p. 51) zitiert werden können.

Zu der Apabhraṃśa-Einlage „Bhāvanā-Svarūpa" (p. 44f.) vergleiche man den Artikel von Madhusūdan C. Modi „*Jayadeva Suri nuṃ Bhāvanā-Sandhi-Prakaraṇa-Kāvya* usw." im Jaina-Yuga, Āṣāḍh-Śravaṇ, saṃvat 1985, p. 469ff. sowie die Ausgabe des in Frage stehenden Apabhraṃśa-Gedichtes in Jaina-Yuga, Māh-Phāgaṇ-Caitra des gleichen Jahrganges, p. 314ff., sowie auch Navatattva-Prakaraṇa Str. 30/31.

Der dritte Teil der Untersuchung beschäftigt sich mit der Sprache, der vierte mit der Metrik der Apabhraṃśa-Texte. Beide fußen auf Jacobis trefflicher Methode und zeugen von guter Beherrschung des Stoffes.

Der fünfte Teil bringt die Texte selbst in einer Herstellung, die fast zuviel mit Konjekturen arbeitet, obwohl zugegeben werden muß, daß sie es mit einer nicht einwandfreien Überlieferung zu tun hat. Auch eine Übersetzung ist beigegeben, die recht nützlich ist. Verschiedene Versehen in Auffassung und Interpretation sind zu berichtigen. So z. B. bezieht sich p. 82. 12 *gamya-agamya* natürlich auf Frauen; p. 82. 13 sind *ghusiṇa* und *tella, candana* und *rasa* einzeln als Dvandva-Glieder zu fassen; p. 82. 14a hat die Sanskrit-Chāyā etwa zu lauten: *prāvṛṣi payaḥ-paṅka-prasaṅga-tyaktaṃ*(?) *vāñchaty acchidrabhavana-sthalaṃ labdhum*; p. 87. 63e ist zu umschreiben: *tasmāt paramārtheṇa Rasaṇaḥ paraṃ mad-vikārasya hetu,* wobei *param* (vgl. die Prakrit Bedeutung) durch „nur", *vikāra-* durch „sinnliche Erregung" (Jaina-t. t.) wiederzugeben ist; p. 88. 76 und 98 Note ist das erste *pratyeka-* im allgemeinen Sinne („jeder") zu fassen, wodurch sich die Note erübrigt; p. 90. 92b ist zu umschreiben: *svarge pi gajaśva-kurkurā bhavanti.*

Zum Beginne der Sthūlabhadra-Kathā p. 100, 2 hätte die Parallelstelle von Hemacandras Pariśiṣṭa-Parvan (VII. 15—18) herangezogen werden müssen, aus der sich klar ergibt, daß *patta* hier *pātra* (*bhājana*) ist und daß der von dem *muni-pātra-kalpa-jala* benetzte der spätere Minister Kalpaka selber ist, dessen Name so erklärt wird.

P. 104. 39 gibt das *saṃcāru* des Originals einen guten Sinn (cp. Prakrit *saṃcāra*); p. 112. 99 hätte *micchā me ḍukkadaṃ* mit „null und nichtig (also: vergeben) sei mein Vergehen" (nicht wie in Fußnote auf p. 122) erklärt werden müssen.

Es folgt ein gleichfalls nach Jacobis Muster knapp und sauber gearbeitetes Glossar, das dann und wann (gottlob) die Volkssprachen konsultiert, sowie einige Anhänge mit Ausgaben von Sanskrit- und Alt-Gujarat-Paralleltexten, die lobenswerten Mut und Fleiß verraten. Den Schluß bildet ein Literatur-Verzeichnis.

Die ganze Untersuchung bildet einen soliden Beitrag zur Kenntnis der mittelindischen und früh-neuindischen Sprachen und Literaturen. Es ist zu wünschen, daß mehr Texte dieser Art erschlossen werden, um für den Aufbau einer historischen Grammatik und für eine umfassende Darstellung der Literatur- und Kulturgeschichte des Arisch-Indischen eine zuverlässige Grundlage zu schaffen.

K. R. Norman

A Critical Pāli Dictionary. Begun by V. Trenckner. Vol. II, 7:

Inda-ugghāṭima. Vol. II, 8: *ugghāṭīyati-udaka-sakuṇika.* Continuing the Work of D. Andersen and H. Smith. Editor-in-Chief: L. Alsdorf†. Kopenhagen: The Royal Danish Academy of Sciences and Letters; Kopenhagen: Munksgaard 1971/73. S. 297-392. 4°.—Bespr. von K.R. Norman, Cambridge U.K.

The first fascicle of Volume II (comprising the vowels *Ĭ—O*) of A Critical Pāli Dictionary (= CPD) appeared in 1960. With the publication of Fascicle 7 (*Inda — ugghāṭima*) in 1971 and Fascicle 8 (*ugghāṭiyati — udaka-sakuṇika*) in 1973, the contributors being W.B. Bollée, C. Caillat, R. Handurukande, H. Kopp, and E. Pauly, the volume is now more than half completed.

These fascicles, like the earlier ones, are based upon an excellent foundation of textual criticism, semantic investigation, and philological accuracy. There was a tendency in earlier fascicles to collect together vast quantities of material and leave it to users to sort out for themselves. This has now been eliminated, and the material is carefully arranged in the presumed order of semantic development, making it much more valuable, and at the same time easier to use. Occasionally an improved translation can be suggested, e.g. (a) *ucchiṭṭha-geha* (p. 350b) 'a house that has been lived in' should rather be translated, on the lines of the other compounds of *ucchiṭṭha-*, 'a house that has been polluted (because others have used it and abandoned it)'; (b) *utuveramaṇī* (368a) is not 'whose menstruation period is over' but 'abstinence from, i.e. cessation of, menstruation', and with the post-position *pati* at Sn 291 it amplifies *tamhā samayā* and means '(except at that time) about the cessation of the menstrual period'. Occasionally the English of the translations is rather quaint, e.g. (a) s. v. *Indagopaka* (298b) 'lady-fly' for 'lady-bird'; (b) s. v. *ujjhita* (358a) 'like a (glowing coal) jumped out'; (c) s. v. *ukkujjati* (334a) 'by turning it upside down for, i.e. against, him'. Occasionally one might differ in analysis or interpretation, e.g. (a) s.v. *utu* (366a) it scarcely seems possible that the word can be used in all three genders. The neuter *utūni*, in an *uddāna* verse (S IV 231, 17), seems likely to be an Eastern masculine nominative plural in *-ni*. What seems to be a feminine form at Th 529 is more likely to be a masculine plural, since the metre demands *utū*; (b) s. v. *iva* (311a) we are told that *-aṁ + iva* > *-aṁ ñeva* or *-añ ñeva*. The existence of *ñ-*, however, shows clearly the earlier presence of *y-*, but since there is no hint that **yiva* ever existed, it seems more likely that we are here dealing with *yeva*. In the same article (311b) the development *-i+iva*> *-êva* is quoted. This may be a genuine change, with the *-ī-/-e-* alternation sometimes found in nouns, e.g. BHS *vīra*/Pāli *vera* 'enmity', but it is more likely that we have *-i+eva*> —'*eva*. Just as *iva* can be used in Sanskrit and Pāli as an emphatic particle (=*eva*), so conversely *eva* and *yeva* are used in the sense of *iva*. Confirmation of this can be seen in Ardha-Māgadhī *visam eva* (Uttarādhyayana-sūtra, XVII. 20), glossed *viṣam iva*.

As in earlier fascicles, all head-words and many compounds are supplied with an etymology, but this is frequently no more than the Sanskrit equivalent, without explanation of anomalies, e.g. (a) s. v. *uṇṇata* (363a) we find (sa. *unnata*], but no hint that *ṇṇ* is perhaps an analogical extension from *paṇata*; (b) s. v. *ukkaṭṭhita* (329b) we find [sa. *utkvathita*] and a reference to Geiger § 42.2, which, however, merely asks 'Wie erklärt sich hier *ṭṭh*?' Sometimes an alternative etymology can be suggested, e.g. (a) s. v. *indagŭ* (298a) 'man' we find [sa. **indra-ga*?] with no suggestion of what this might mean. It might be worthwhile considering a derivation<skt. **Indraka* (cf. Pāli *antagū*/BHS *antaka*), and reviving the old etymology which connected *Indra* with Greek ἀνηe (see M. Mayrhofer, Etymologisches Wörterbuch des Altindischen, Vol. I, p. 89); (b) s. v. *ujjhāyati* (357b) 'to become indignant or irritated', it seems more likely that, despite BHS *avadhyāyati*, this is not [1]*jhāyati*<skt. *dhyāyati*, but [2]*jhāyati*<skt. *kṣāyati*; (c) s. v. *Irubbeda* (310b) we find a reference to Trenckner's suggestion that it is formed in analogy with *Yajubbeda*. This, however, still leaves the problem of *ir-* to explain, and it seems more likely that the development was *Ṛgveda*>**Irgveda* (with the change *ṛ-*>*ir-*, as opposed to *ṛ-*>*ri*, e.g. *ṛṣi*>*risi*)>**Irvveda*>**Iruvveda—Irubbeda*; (d) s.v. *ujju* (353b) we might see a comparable development< **urju*<*ṛju*.

As one uses these two fascicles, a certain unevenness and inconsistency between the various articles becomes apparent, arising no doubt from the plurality of authors, the long period of gestation, and the various reworkings to which the material has been subjected. Abbreviations are not always standardized, e.g. (a) the reviewer's translations of Th and Thī are variously referred to as Norman, Elders' Verses I and II (p. 358a), or Norman, Th Translation (360a); (b) Miss I.B. Horner's translation of Vin as

Horner, SBB XIV (382a), or Horner, Book of Disc. IV (386a). Sometimes the cross-referencing has gone awry, e.g. (a) s.v. *anuggahāya* (CPD, Vol. I, 183b) there is a reference to *ugganhāti*. There is, however, no mention of *(an-)uggahāya* s. v. *ugganhāti* (339b), nor s. v. *uggahāyati* (342b); (b) s. v. *uttiṭṭha* (382a) there is a reference to *ucchiṭṭha*, but no reference under the latter (350b) to the former; (c) s. v. *Inda-ssama* (301b) there is a reference to *Indasama*, but no reference under the latter (301a) to *Inda-ssama*. Those using E[e] (1) of Vv will be surprised to find no mention of the reading at Vv 772 s. v. *Inda-sama*, but they are given no hint that they should refer to *-ssama*.

CPD is not a concordance, and we cannot, therefore, expect to find every reference, or even every important reference, for every Pāli word. It is, however, essential to have an accurate survey of the types of text in which every word occurs, and especially a reference to its earliest attestation. Sometimes an earlier or more interesting reference than those listed can be given, e.g. (a) *ukkaṭṭh'-ukkaṭṭha* (329b) is not quoted from a Buddhaghosa commentary, but it also occur at Sp 704,3; (b) *ibha* (307a) 'elephant' is quoted only from grammarians and the late Jina-c, but it also occurs at Sv-pṭ (E[e]) I 388, 10-11, as is stated s. v. *ibbha*; (c) *isivāta-parivāta* (316b) is called a (post-canonical) cliché, but the references given (Vibh 247, 17 Nidd I 474, 24) belie this statement. Perhaps late-canonical is meant?

The printing and presentation of these two fascicles is up to the usual very high standards of CPD. Usage to date has revealed only two misprints overlooked during the very accurate proofreading: (a) the omission of the hyphen in *ukkhitta-cīvara* (336a) (b) the omission of the references (Vin I 211, 32 239, 36) s. v. *ukka-piṇḍaka* (331b).

The points commented upon above are all of a very minor nature, and in no way detract from the immense value of these two fascicles. Such defects and inconsistencies as do occur are likely to be less frequent in future, now that the Editor-in-Chief has taken over the task of personally preparing the manuscript for the press. All those working in the fields of Pāli and Buddhist Studies will without doubt join the reviewer in giving an unqualified welcome to these latest fascicles of CPD, and in looking forward to the appearance of the remainder of Volume II.

K.R. Norman

A Critical Pāli Dictionary. Begun by V. Trenckner. Vol. II, 9: *udaka-saṅkhāta—upakkama.* Continuing the Work of D. Andersen and H. Smith. Editor-in-Chief: L. Alsdorf†. Kopenhagen: The Royal Danish Academy of Sciences and Letters; Kopenhagen: Munksgaard 1975. S. 393—432 4⁰. Bespr. von K.R. Norman, Cambridge.

The ninth fascicle of Volume II of CPD (*udakasaṅkhāta—upakkama*), dated 1975 but not received until April 1976, is based upon contributions by W.B. Bollée, H. Kopp, and the Calcutta CPD Centre under the Government of India, whose first contribution to CPD this is. As in the case of the eighth fascicle, the manuscript was prepared for the press by L. Alsdorf. Such preparation by the Editor-in-Chief, although providing uniformity of treatment, also imposes a cover of anonymity, so that users of the fascicle do not know whom to praise or blame for individual features. Only the publication of 'Pali Miscellanies' in Volume I of "Studien zur Indologie und Iranistik" (not referred to in this fascicle) tells us that it was Alsdorf himself who made the brilliant suggestion that *uddhaṁ-sarā* (p. 417b) means 'transmigration'. We cannot tell who found the etymologies which have been suggested for *udrabhati/udrahati* (427a) unconvincing (but could not suggest anything better), or was unconvinced by the reviewer's suggestion referred to s. v. *upakūḷita* (432b). The suggestion itself is not quoted, which could cause confusion to readers if it is altered in a second edition of Elders' Verses II.

Similarly, s. v. *uddhacca* (418b) we find the statement 'PED wrong', without quotation of the error. A second edition of PED is in preparation, in which the error will doubtless be corrected, but even the correction will still be condemned by this sweeping statement. Confusion may also arise from certain inconsistencies in cross-referencing, e.g. (a) s. v. *udaka-rohana* (Vol. II.8, 392a) the suggestion was accepted that the correct reading was *-orohana.* There is, however, no mention of this emendation s. vv. *-orohaṇa* or *-orohana* (395b); (b) s. v. *udañcani* (396b) H. Smith's emendation of *udañcani* for *udakañcana* is quoted for Dhp-a (new ed.) I 95, 14, but there is no entry for *udakañcana* to explain that the word is a w(rong) r(eading), nor in fact does the word actually occur at Dhp-a (first ed.) I 113,8 (=new ed. I 95, 14); (c) s. v. *udañcani* (396b) *udañjaniko* is quoted as a v. l. for *uddekaniko*, and is said to be a w. r. for *udañcaniko*, but there is no entry for *udañjanika*, nor is the v. l. quoted s. v. *uddekanika* (414a).

Comment is called for on some words, e.g. (a) *udarâvadehakaṁ* (401b) is called an indeclinable, but *(pheṇ-)uddehakaṁ* (415b) an adverb, as is also *udara-pūraṁ* (401a). Since the Sanskrit grammarians classify *-pūraṁ* as a *ṇamul*-type absolutive, it would seem preferable to call all the verbal forms in *-aṁ* or *-akaṁ* either *ṇamul*-s or indeclinables; (b) s. v. *uddha* (416a) *uddhehi vatthehi* at Ja IV 154,15 (a mistake for 15*, since it is a verse) is said to be a w. r. in Eᵉ, and Cᶜ and Bᵉ are referred to for the correct reading *suddhehi*. The reading in Eᵉ, however, is a misprint, not a w. r., and the writer of the entry has overlooked the correct reading at Ja IV 144,6 (as has also F. Edgerton, *Buddhist Hybrid Sanskrit Dictionary*, s. v. *ūrdhva*); (c) s. v. *uddhata* (421 b) the treatment of *ut'uddhata* is not clear. It seems that a different interpretation is being proposed from that given earlier s. v. *uddhaṭa* (Vol. II.8, 367a), but since the same translation 'drawn out by the seasons' is given for both entries the situation is confusing. The reading with *-t-* suggests that *uddhata* (=*ud*+*hata*) should be taken in the same sense as *hata*, i.e. 'beaten'='washed (in the Indian style against a rock)', rather than 'worn out', but in Sanskrit and elsewhere in Pāli *uddhata* seems not to be used in this sense. Turner (CDIAL 2009) quotes a number of New Indo-Aryan forms derived from *uddhaṭa*, with the meanings 'unravelled', 'undone (of seams, etc.)' 'ripped', 'split', and this might well be the idea here.

Some of the English in the translations sounds rather quaint, and is even misleading in places, e.g. (a) s. v. *uda-bindu* (397b) 'waterdrop'; (b) s. v. *udaka-sādhāraṇa* (393b) 'joint with water'; (c) s. v. *unnat'unnata* (428a) 'knot for knot elevated'; (d) s. v. *unnāmi-ninnāmi* (*n*) (429a) 'raised and bent' is not a synonym for 'rising and sinking' which is given as an alternative; (e) s. v. *uddiyati* (405b) '*ss* misread sinh. *yy*' and s. v. *uddhumāyikā* (427a) 'singh. *k* misread *t*' presumably mean 'sinh. *yy* misread as *ss*' and 'sinh. *k* misread as *t*' respectively.

Although CPD is not intended to be a Concordance or an Encyclopaedia, the earliest attestation of a word is essential, and the imparting of a minimum of background knowledge is advisable e.g. (a) s. v. (*uddeheti*) (415b) an explanation of *pheṇ'uddehakaṃ* by *pheṇaṃ uddehetvā* is quoted from the late Vismmhṭ. The same compound is explained by *pheṇaṃ uddihitvā* at Mp IV 65, 12, but there is no entry for (*uddihati*); (*b*) s. v. *udumbara* (407a) the statement 'the ~ is supposed to have no flowers' is not very helpful for anyone coming across the common statement about something being as rare as an *udumbara* flower, and the inclusion of a note about the flowering habits of fig-trees would have been helpful.

Usage to date has revealed only a few misprints: (a) 15 for 15*, s. v. *uddha* (416a), as mentioned above; (b) haughthy for haughty, s. v. *uddhata* (421b); (c) he for the, s. v. *uddhacca-vamana* (420b) (d) the omission of the reference M I 306, 12 s. v. *udrabhati*/*udrahati* (427a). Otherwise the printing, presentation, and proof-reading are up to the very high standards we have come to expect from CPD. The very minor points mentioned above in no way detract from the sound and solid basis of philological accuracy which has made CPD an indispensable tool for all those working in the fields of Pāli and Buddhist studies.

Louis Renou

Heinrich Lüders, *Varuṇa*. 1: Varuṇa und die Wasser. Aus dem Nachlaß hg. von Ludwig Alsdorf. 8° 337p. Vandenhoeck & Ruprecht, Göttingen 1951. DM 28.60

Cet ouvrage, qui représente l'activité principale de M.L. durant les dernières années de sa vie, a subi plus d'une tribulation avant de nous parvenir. Le manuscrit des tomes 1 et 2 (les seuls achevés d'un ouvrage qui devait en comporter trois) avait été gravement endommagé; il a fallu combler les lacunes, souvent considérables, à l'aide de notes de cours ou de brouillons anciens. Aidé de plusieurs collaborateurs, M. Alsdorf, l'indianiste bien connu, s'est attelé à cette tâche ingrate avec tout le soin et la compétence qu'on attendait de lui. Il a complété les références, ajouté les citations sanskrites en bas de page; bref, nous avons grâce à lui la pensée du grand indianiste allemand sous une forme aussi voisine qu'il était possible de la rédaction que, de son vivant, il aurait pu souhaiter lui donner.

L'ouvrage concerne un des problèmes centraux — peut-être *le* problème central — du védisme: le problème de Varuṇa, qui n'a cessé depuis les origines des études védiques de susciter hypothèses après hypothèses.

La recherche de M.L. (pour autant qu'on peut la juger d'ensemble d'après ce seul vol.) part du principe qu'il existe une association essentielle entre VARUṆA et les eaux, étant entendu que ≪les caux≫ ne sont pas seulement (ni même, préférablement) le milieu qui nous est familier: rivières et mers, lacs at pluies, mais d'abord et surtout le milieu ≪cosmique≫, qui, on le sait, est toujours présent à l'esprit des *kavi* du Véda. M.L. insiste, avec une parfaite légitimité, il me semble, sur le fait que les eaux régies par VARUṆA sont les eaux ≪célestes≫ bien plus souvent que les eaux terrestres, en sorte que cette divinité peut les habiter en même temps qu'elle réside au ciel. Un même mot, *samudrá*, désigne selon lui, à la fois l'océan circulaire (notion qui sera précisée dans la cosmographie épique et purāṇique, mais que M.L. a le mérite d'identifier dés le Véda), l'océan ≪indien≫, enfin l'océan céleste. De même le mot *sindhú* note aussi bien les fleuves sillonnant la terre que ceux du ciel, et spécialement celui qui marque la frontière entre les deux domaines. Aux ≪spet fleuves≫ ou plutôt au –fleuve septuple– du ciel correspond l'océan situé derrière le ciel visible.

De proche en proche, comme il est presque inévitable dans ce domaine à la fois flottant et plein d'interpénétrations qu'est la mythologie du Véda, l'a. est amené à définir d'autres zones mythiques qui lui paraissent présenter la même ambivalence ou multivalence. Ainsi il découvre deux registres du *soma*: à côté du *soma* rituel, le *soma* qui monte au ciel et vient séjourner dans les eaux célestes: les fleuves ≪du ciel≫ sont conçus comme un écoulement de la mer de *soma* sise au plus haut du ciel. De même, il y a deux registres pour le soleil: à côté du soleil céleste, le soleil caché dans les eaux. Enfin la mer céleste, où sont contenus les eaux, le *soma*, les étoiles, est enfermée dans un rocher (*ádri*): c'est précisément ce rocher qu'INDRA combat lorsqu'il pourfend le ≪démon≫ VṚTRA: c'est le barrage des eaux célestes, qui avaient été avalées par VṚTRA.

Cette importance des thèmes cosmologiques, ce double plan ≪terrestre≫et≪céleste≫, étaient des notions connues depuis longtemps dans leurs grandes lignes; BERGAIGNE notamment, dans son ouvrage sur la *Religion védique*, les avait utilisées de place en place. Mais il faut reconnaître que M.L. apporte une démonstration entièrement renouvelée par la rigueur et l'ampleur de la méthode;

il la confirme d'une masse énorme de références, de déductions qui lui assurent des assises solides, on voudrait croire définitives.

Chemin faisant, il est conduit à réviser maintes traductions de mots ou de versets; son attitude est passablement critique à l'égard de ses devanciers. Sur ce point l'ouvrage sera d'une utilité considérable aux étudiants du Véda, et il sera naturellement indispensable qu'en fin du tome 2 un index des mots et des passages cités vienne rendre possible le maniement de ce livre fort touffu.

La tendance de M. L. ne tient aucun compte, on le voit, des efforts «réalistes» qui ont été faits dans les études védiques depuis quelque quinze ans, interprétations sociologiques et autres. Ceci est d'autant plus frappant que le tour d'esprit de M. L., dans l'ensemble de son oeuvre, était fort éloginé de celui d'un mythographe «classique», à la manière de MAX MÜLLER ou de KUHN. Il faut y voir le produit d'une réflexion délibérée. D'autre part, le gros de l'ouvrage était pensé, sinon rédigé, probablement dès 1936; en tout cas, les références bibliographiques (qui ne sont d'ailleurs pas fréquentes) ne vont guère au-delà de cette date; elles se fondent surtout sur OLDENBERG et GELDNER (la suite encore inédite de la traduction de GELDNER ayant heureusement pu être utilisée par l'a.).

Je ne suis pas de ceux qui reprocheront à M. L. sa mythologie cosmologique. Certes la vérité sur les mythes védiques risque d'être «multiple», en ce sens que plusieurs explications sont simultanément valables pour les grandes figures divines du Véda. Mais je pense qu'il y a plus de vérité essentielle dans la perspective M. L. (même si elle est sociologiquement ou historiquement moins «intéressante») que dans des approches toutes différentes qu'on a pu tenter.

Une objection vient cependant à l'esprit: on considère d'habitude la liaison entre VARUṆA et les Eaux comme secondaire, parce qu'elle n'apparaît pas (du moins à première vue) dans les Hymnes les plus archaïques et qu'elle prend au contraire de plus en plus d'importance durant la période post-ṛgvédique de la littérature ancienne. C'est vrai, mais l'objection est valable surtout quand on envisage les eaux comme un milieu «terrestre»: elle l'est beaucoup moins si les eaux sont un symbole «céleste». En outre, il semble bien que M. L. fasse assez bon marché de l'évolution interne du Véda à laquelle d'autres savants ont attaché une importance peut-être excessive. Il lui arrive d'expliquer les données védiques en fonction de thèmes purāṇiques ou épiques. C'est un retour partiel aux méthodes des *Vedische Studien*, dont s'inspire l'a. encore quand il refuse d'expliquer le Véda en liaison avec l'indo-européen: aucune représentation religieuse ou linguistique attribuable à l'indo-européen, voire à l'indo-iranien, n'est discutée dans ce livre; la discussion, d'ailleurs fort intéressante, sur gr. διιπετης (p. 141), repose sur un fait de convergence, non d'héritage. D'ailleurs M. L. est animé par le souci très net de fixer ce que telle divinité signifiait pour «l-Indien védique», nullement de retrouver ce qu'elle avait pu signifier à ses origines pré-historiques. Cette attitude, évidemment valable en soi, est poursuivie avec beaucoup de rigueur tout au long de l'ouvrage.

Toutefois, dans les pages d'introduction, l'a., après avoir résumé (pour les rejeter toutes) les hypothèses qu'on a formulées sur l'essence de VARUṆA, donne certaines indications sur la manière dont il entend l'être propre de ce dieu et la nature de son rapport avec les Eaux. Autant qu'on puisse voir, il s'oriente vers la notion de VARUṆA comme «dieu du serment» (comme le laissaient entrevoir déjà certains passages de son mémoire de 1917 *Eine arische Anschauung über den Vertragsbruch*). VARUṆA serait le protecteur du *satyá* ou du «vrai» (attesté sous la foi du serment), le *satyá* étant lui-même identique au *ṛtá*: car tel est la signification que, d'une manière très résolue, M. L. assigne à ce terme si controversé (cf. déjà l'article posthume *Die magische Kraft der Wahrheit im alten Indien*, *Z. D. M. G.*, 1944, p. 1). J'avoue que c'est là un point qui me gêne, et je ne suis pas disposé à éliminer le sens «cosmique» de *ṛtá*, «ordre» ou «cours» des phénomènes, tout en reconnaissant qu'il n'y a pas du point de vue indien antinomie ni même différence fondamentale entre les notions d'«ordre» et de «vérité». C'est, ajoute M. L., par l'effet de son association avec le serment que VARUṆA est Roi, qu'il est Juge, qu'il détient son rôle bien connu de pourchasseur d'impies, c.-à-d., proprement, de «menteurs» (*drùhvan*). Quant à MITRA, l'a. admet l'interprétation comme divinité du «contrat» et souligne justement, à ce propos, l'importance des divinités abstraites dans le Véda. Enfin la longue association de VARUṆA et des Eaux s'explique par le rôle de l'eau comme instrument privilégié du serment (cf. l'ordalie par l'eau, etc.).

Il n'est pas douteux que l'ouvrage de M. L. marque une époque dans les études védiques; il met le point final à tout un aspect des recherches qui avait prévalu au 19e s., et il barre la route à des fantaisies plus ou moins aventureuses. C'est un travail sain et probe, fondé sur un examen précis, exhaustif, des textes. Il sera, il va sans dire, indispensable à consulter pour tout étudiant intéressé aux problèmes védiques.

J. E. SPENCER

VORDERINDIEN: Bharat—Pakistan—Ceylon: Eine Landes- und Kulturkunde. By LUDWIG ALSDORF. 336 pp.; maps, diagrs,. ills., bibliogr., index. Georg Westermann Verlag, Braunschweig, 1955. DM 22.- $9\frac{1}{2} \times 6\frac{1}{2}$ inches.

This volume is another excellent modern geography of the Indian subcontinent. It went to press just at the time of publication of O. H. K. Spate's "India and Pakistan" (*Geogr. Rev.*, Vol. 45, 1955, pp. 436-437) and presents a somewhat later picture than Spate, who completed his writing in 1951. Alsdorf has written for the reader who is content to view India as a geographic realm, divided at the moment into several political units; he has not written of politically separate countries as such. He has in mind a broad comparison of the land and life of the Indian subcontinent with those of Europe exclusive of Soviet Russia. He is attentive to the matters of native growth of culture, and also to the matters of British supervision of India, that make the region different from Europe. Although Alsdorf writes a medium-difficult German, his book is excellently organized and written and is almost as easy to use as Spate's volume, which has its own special problems of language and presentation. There is obviously much less detail in the 336 pages of "Vorderindien" than in the 827 pages of "India and Pakistan," but in view of Alsdorf's clear-cut presentation this is a virtue to the reader who wants a rounded yet succinct treatment. Alsdorf has depended largely on German authorities for many of his interpretations; Spate used few non-English sources.

Alsdorf has balanced his subject matter rather evenly between systematic discussion and regional treatment. A short introduction conjures up all the things India has meant to people everywhere. Thirty two pages are then devoted to the general situation of the component countries and physical units. Some 50 pages treat population distribution, settlement patterns, races, languages, religions, and culture. The last century, one of political regionalism ranging from the British assumption of control over the Sikh portion of northwestern India to the formation of the Maldive Republic, receives 26 pages. An appendix chart gives the flags of the Indian Union, Pakistan, Ceylon, Nepal, Bhutan, and the Maldives, but there are still the Portuguese holdings to complicate the political map further. This section is a concise, orderly treatment of the modern political geography of this part of the world, but it does lack cartographic illustration.

In 50 pages Alsdorf presents a generalized discussion of the economy of India and Pakistan, with a short section on Ceylon. He has kept his text free of statistics and tables for the most part, has used maps where he thought them necessary, and has referred the reader to the statistical appendix for specific data. The longest section of the book, just over 100 pages, is a discussion of the geographic regions, the boundaries of which are presented on a map (p. 178). Alsdorf divides the subcontinent into 21 major regions that appear fairly standard units, and he recognizes but has not cartographically delineated a small number of subregions, whereas Spate recognized 38 first-order regional units and a long list of subregions. Here are summary comments about whole human landscape units rather than details of regional geography, such as one finds in Spate. Alsdorf's summary of the Sind region covers three pages and a half, against the nine pages used by Spate, and his discussion of Tamilnad, the southeastern coastal fringe, occupies a few lines over four pages, as compared with the 50 pages given this area by Spate.

The terminal section of Alsdorf's volume is an excellent statistical summary. Here he presents a wide range of tabular information, much of it hard to come by elsewhere, and wherever possible he has separated it for India, Pakistan, and Ceylon. This section is far more useful than Spate's shorter, earlier, and less inclusive statistical summary. If one is not able to read all the German of the text, this statistical summary alone makes the book well worth consulting.

A selected bibliography of more than 130 items is classified by major subjects. There are fewer maps than one expects from a German geography, but there are a considerable number of excellent, representative photographs. All in all, this volume well maintains the high level of German regional geographies of major parts of the world.

Prof. P. THIEME (Tübngen)

LUDWIG ALSDORF AND VEDIC STUDIES

HE WHO KNEW Ludwig Alsdorf personally could not but recognize that all his endeavours and achievements in the field of Indology rested on a deep personal sympathy with India and the values of Indian culture — a personal sympathy amounting to love. It was not the love of a fanciful enthusiast, but the critical love of a scholar. It was the love of a humanist ready to cross all the boundaries of nationality, religion, and race, capable to discover the beauty and greatness — and to recognize the unavoidable flaws and shortcomings - of human creations in literature and art everywhere and in all their variety, and finding his satisfaction and reward in contributing, within the domain of his studies, to the acknowledgement of the universal truth that 'the proper study of mankind is man'.

Alsdorf's sympathetic interest in India was of an universality not easy to find in any of his contemporaries. Being a specialist in Jaina Apabhraṃśa — and Bauddha Pāli-literature and all the 'middle Indian' languages connected with the development and history of these religious literatures — down from the old dialects recorded on the Aśoka inscriptions —, he took a vivid scholarly interest in modern India too, following in particular the Indian freedom movement and the growth of the young Republic of India with a keen and painstaking sympathy.

Alsdorf's universality of outlook — his 'sarvatomukhatvam', to express it in Sanskrit — with regard to India extended not only from the Indian oldest 'middle ages' up to the most modern times: it reached back into India's hoariest antiquity. Many years of labor did he spend on the Ṛgveda, presenting Veda philology with most valuable contributions, for which the Veda specialist's deep gratitude is due to him.

His greatest achievement in this field is, of course, his edition of the two volumes 'Varuṇa I' (1951) and 'Varuṇa II' (1959) based on manuscripts left by Heinrich Lüders, constituting this eminent German Indologist's Rigvedic heritage. This posthumous edition, literature were expected to appear, and knowledge of this material was correctly judged to be fundamental for the exploration of the history of Indo-Aryan languages and Indo-Aryan literature, especially for studies in the history of Jaina literature. By investigating the appr. 250 Apabhraṃśa stanzas of the Kumārapālapratibodha, Alsdorf was in a position to confirm (and to render more precise) Jacobi's observations on the lexicography and grammar of that stage of Middle Indo-Aryan. As far as grammar was concerned, Alsdorf recognized the difference between the dialect areas of Northern or Classical Apabhraṃśa on the one hand and Gurjara Apabhraṃśa, as used by Haribhadra and Somaprabha, on the other. He also disclosed the interdependence of different stylistic levels and the interspersion of Prakrit words by these authors. Notwithstanding the efforts Professor Schubring and Alsdorf made to obtain any manuscript of the Kumārapālapratibodha or at least the single manuscript the printed edition was based on, it was impossible to revise the text and to check the readings of the editio princeps. Alsdorf's knowledge of Apabhraṃśa nevertheless enabled him to emend the text and to restore the original wording in many difficult passages. In his interpretation of the text, Alsdorf pointed out Somaprabha's characteristic way of representing dogmatic holdings and his intellectual relations with earlier and contemporary authors. Moreover, Alsdorf presented in his thesis an exhaustive analysis of two tales which are interesting with regard to Somaprabha's position in literary history: the Jīva-manaḥ-karaṇa-saṃlāpa-kathā and the legend of Sthūlabhadra. Alsdorf followed up the development of the Sthūlabhadra legend through the successive layers of language, namely Prakrit (including the version contained in Bhadreśvara's Kathāvalī which has not been edited until today), Sanskrit, Apabhraṃśa, and Gujarati, focussing attention on the special features of the story as displayed by Somaprabha's version.

Through his study of the Kumārapālapratibodha, Alsdorf was excellently prepared for the far more ambitious project of studying the Harivaṃśapurāṇa of the Digambara author Puṣpadanta. Whereas the material formed by Somaprabha's Apabhraṃśa stanzas can be said to be limited and easy to survey, the Harivaṃśapurāṇa forms part of the immense corpus of the Jaina Universal History which had received little treatment by European scholars when Alsdorf entered this field in 1928. At that time Alsdorf was shown a manuscript of the said text (lent to Hermann Jacobi from the Deccan College through the kindness of Muni Jinavijaya). The Harivaṃśapurāṇa or Nemicarita, as it is called by the Śvetāmbaras, contains the story of the 22nd Tīrthaṃkara and of the heroes Kṛṣṇa, Balarāma, and Jarāsandha (i.e. the ninth triad: Vāsudeva, Baladeva, and Prativāsudeva respectively). It forms chapters 81 to 92 of the Mahāpurāṇa, wholly composed in Apabhraṃśa, by the kavi Puṣpadanta between 959 and 965 A.D. It proved again extremely difficult to obtain manuscripts sufficient to restore the text, and Alsdorf would not have been successful had it not been for the substantial help of two Indian scholars, P.L. Vaidya and, in particular, Hiralal Jain, who (being himself a Digambara Jaina) had access to the important library of Karanja and supported Alsdorf's undertaking during the latter's stay in India from 1930 to 1932. Thus Alsdorf could utilize at least three valuable manuscripts which, as he discovered, represented two different recensions of the text, one of them distinctly earlier than the other and nearer to the presumable original. This discovery was confirmed by the corresponding readings of the entirely different manuscripts used by P. L. Vaidya, when he constituted afterwards the text of the entire Mahāpurāṇa.[5] Alsdorf's monograph — which gained him the venia legendi (teaching licence) when submitted to the Faculty of Arts of the Friedrich-Wilhelms-Universität in Berlin in 1935 as his

5. The Mahāpuraṇa or Tisaṭṭhimahāpurisaguṇālaṃkāra of Puṣpadanta, critically ed. by P.L. Vaidya. Vols. I-III = Manikchand Digambara Jaina Granthamālā 37.41.42, Bombay 1937-1941. For the third volume Alsdorf had contributed a Devanāgarī transcription of his edition of the Harivaṃśapurāṇa and an English extract of his treatise. The first volume was reviewed by Alsdorf in OLZ 40, 1939, 593-611 (Bibl. No. 24). In this article Alsdorf warned, that in spite of the high value of the earlier recension the reliability of the respective manuscripts should not be overestimated. Scrutinizing the various readings, he proposed a number of convincing emendations. He also pointed out an interesting parallel between the Mahāpurāṇa (7, 20, 11 sqq. and 8, 2, 6 sqq.) and Hemacandra's Triṣaṣṭiśalākāpuruṣacaritra (1, 3, 4 sqq. and 1, 3, 104 sqq.). This was an instance where the two texts had a common source which was not used by either Jinasena or Śilaṅka. It showed how difficult the question of the interrelation of the different versions of the Universal History really was.

in 1902, before many more Apabhraṃśa texts had come to light. In a smaller article ("Middle Indian Miscellanies") Alsdorf referred again to the subject.[10]

While examining the literary parallels to the Harivaṃśapurāṇa, Alsdorf discovered the special importance of Saṅghadāsa's Vasudevahiṇḍi as a Jaina version of Guṇāḍhya's Bṛhatkathā. He also realized that the Vasudevahiṇḍi was a valuable piece of Prakrit literature, written in a cultivated style "far from being concise or dry; it presents us with a vivid, characteristic and highly interesting picture of a living language", as he himself described his impression in "The Vasudevahiṇḍi, a Specimen of Archaic Jaina-Māhārāṣṭrī" (1935).[11] This article, dealing mainly with some "striking features and peculiarities" of the language of the text, was meant to be "a kind of preliminary notice", preceding a monograph the title of which had already been mentioned in the Habilitationsschrift as "Die Jainaversion der Bṛhatkathā".[12] While that undertaking was left unfinished, Alsdorf returned to the subject of the Vasudevahiṇḍi on several occasions. In his article on "Zwei neue Belege zur 'indischen Herkunft' von 1001 Nacht"[13] he presented text and translation of a passage of the Cārudatta-carita (Vasudevahiṇḍi p. 146, 5 — p. 147, 26) and of the Kokkāsa episode (Vh. p. 61,25 — p. 64,2) — the latter in comparison with the corresponding passage of the Āvaśyaka ṭīkā — pointing out that these texts are to be looked upon as the earliest sources of the respective tales in the Arabian Nights. Three years later, in "A New Version of the Agaḍadatta Story",[14] he compared meticulously the wording of Vasudevahiṇḍi pp. 39,27 foll. with the parallel version in Devendra's Uttarādhyayana commentary, emphasizing the value of the former as the earlier rendering. Alsdorf pointed out that — apart from archaic features of the language — the veḍhas occurring in the Vasudevahiṇḍi can be interpreted as an indication of the antiquity of the text. Alsdorf

10. Bibl. No. 48.
11. Bibl. No. 20, cp. especially p. 321 = Kl. Schr. p. 58.
12. Cp. p. 35 of the "Habilitationsschrift". The announcement was repeated in a paper which Alsdorf presented to the international conference of orientalists held in Rome in 1937. On that occasion Alsdorf discussed Budhasvāmin's Bṛhatkathāślokasaṃgraha in the light of the new evidence presented by the Vasudevahiṇḍi (Bibl. No. 22).
13. Bibl. No. 49.
14. Bibl. No. 23.

has treated the veḍhas extensively in the Friedrich Weller Felicitation Volume, published in 1954.[15]

Jaina cosmography was also a subject in which Alsdorf had become interested through the medium of the Harivaṃśapurāṇa and the Vasudevahiṇḍi. Expounding the digvijaya of a Cakravartin as depicted in Jaina literature, Alsdorf elucidated the rôle of the vidyādharas who, as demonstrated by him, were adopted by the Jainas from Guṇāḍhya's Bṛhatkathā and included into their cosmological system (1938).[16]

In a further study of Jaina cosmography published in 1947,[17] Alsdorf followed up the events connected with the birth of a Jina, as described by the various lines of tradition, having in view mainly the description given in the fifth part of the Jambuddīvapaṇṇatti, i.e. the janmakalyāṇa.

In his later years, Alsdorf (having succeeded Walther Schubring as a professor in ordinary and Director of the Seminar für Kultur und Geschichte Indiens at the University of Hamburg in 1950) started penetrating researches on the Jaina Canon. Striving consistently for a better understanding of the genuine thought of the most ancient testimonies of the Jaina creed, he focussed attention on the so-called "Senioren" (earliest texts) of the canon. In the course of a few years he published four articles on selected chapters of the Uttarādhyayana, namely chapter nos. 22 (1955),[18] 13 (1957),[19] 9 (1962),[20] and (combined in the "Uttarajjhāyā Studies", 1962) nos. 10, 15, and 12.[21] Investigations into chapter nos. 24, 36, 33, 26, 28, 30, and 34 — all of them including passages composed in the āryā metre — were added in 1966, forming the treatise on "The Āryā Stanzas of the Uttarajjhāyā".[22] These metrical studies were not pursued by Alsdorf for their own sake but in order to obtain a criterion for distinguishing between the earlier and the later textual layers which were often mixed in one and the same

15. Bibl. No. 27.
16. Bibl. No. 21.
17. Bibl. No. 25.
18. Bibl. No. 28.
19. Bibl. No. 29.
20. Bibl. No. 31.
21. Bibl. No. 32. The treatment of Uttarajjhāyā chapter 15, i.e. of the sabhikkhū stanzas, was accompanied by a new edition, with explanatory notes, of its parallel in the Dasaveyāliyasutta chapter 10.
22. Bibl. No. 12.

piece of literature. As the metrical features of the oldest specimens of Jaina poetry became partly obsolete in later times, the texts were subject to misinterpretations and corruptions of various kinds, such as false spellings and interpretations. That the correct understanding of the metrical shape is very helpful for the reconstruction of the original wording of the ancient texts, was exemplified by Alsdorf *inter alia* by his treatment of the vaitālīya/aupacchandasaka stanzas of Uttarādhyayana chapter no. 10 and by his critical edition, translation, and annotation of Sūyagaḍaṅga I 4 (Itthiparinnā) which was composed in the āryā metre of the earlier type.[23]

In his study in the history of vegetarianism,[24] Alsdorf characterized the Jaina concept of ahiṃsā in comparison with the respective ideas of the Buddhists and the Hindus. In this connection, Alsdorf examined again two chapters of the Uttarādhyayana (nos. 12 and 25), proving them to bear witness of the mental attitude of the ancient Jaina ascetics: criticism of the brahmanical cult of sacrificing was indeed a strong motive for the opposite endeavour of the Jainas (as well as of the Buddhists), the crucial point being, however, that the Brahmanical sacrifice was felt to form part of an antiquated ritualistic system that had become rigid and shallow and was ripe to be overthrown by the promulgators of the "real Brahma", that is the ideals of Jainism (and Buddhism as well).[25]

In a series of lectures held at the Collège de France in 1965,[26] Alsdorf summed up the actual position and the future tasks of researches on Jainism. After pointing out the great number of parallels between early Jainism and early Buddhism, Alsdorf underlined the general importance of the tradition as handed down by the Jainas for a study of the development of both religions. He demonstrated the need of a comparative investigation into the respective literary sources. Choosing as an example the field of metrics, especially the earlier and the later types of the āryā metre,

23. On two later occasions, Alsdorf referred again to the vaitālīya metre, also known as māgadhikā: (i) in his Études Jaina, p. 24 sq. (Bibl. No. 13, with respect to Utt. niryukti stanzas 137 sq.), (ii) in an article (Bibl. No. 159) dealing with two passages of the Maṇipaticarita, where Alsdorf was able to restore 15 stanzas composed in this rare metre and showing also the characteristics of the Māgadhī language.
24. Bibl. No. 10.
24. Cp. especially pp. 47-49.
26. Bibl. No. 13.

Alsdorf demonstrated the possibilities of determining, with the help of the metre, the chronological order of the texts. He also suggested that further critical editions of the ancient texts — including the rare old commentaries (niryuktis, cūrṇis, and ṭīkās)[27] — should be prepared. Alsdorf emphasized that it is these old commentaries which deserve to be analyzed extensively, following the course Ernst Leumann had set out, when he began surveying the Āvaśyaka tradition.[28] Concerning the layer of the niryuktis, Alsdorf stressed that the study of parallel versions as preserved by the Digambaras were not to be neglected.[29]

In three of his last articles, Alsdorf actually took up the subject of the exegetical scriptures of Jainism. He directed attention to a passage of the Āvaśyaka cūrṇi, unnoticed till then (p. 35 of the Cūrṇi print). This passage showed that its author, while stating that the 12th aṅga of the Jaina canon was still a regular object of study, betrayed his complete ignorance of that long-lost text.[30] In a further article, Alsdorf explained the nikṣepa, a method of approaching a subject by means of fixed viewpoints, which was frequently used in scholastic Jaina literature, particularly in the niryuktis. He illustrated the nikṣepa technique by quotations

27. Invited by Muni Puṇyavijaya and co-operative Indian friends, Alsdorf himself had photographed in 1951 valuable palm-leaf manuscripts in the Jaina Bhandars of Jaisalmer, Patan, and Cambay for the purpose of preparing new editions of the texts. For my edition of a part of the Oghaniryukti (cp. Piṇḍ'esaṇā, Wiesbaden 1973), Alsdorf made available to me the photographs of two of these manuscripts, and he helped other scholars in the same way. — Describing his journey to Jaisalmer in the Schubring Felicitation Volume, Alsdorf highly appreciated the preparatory work which Muni Puṇyavijaya had done for the project of a critical edition of the complete Śvetāmbara Canon (Bibl. No. 26).
28. Cp. Ernst Leumann, Übersicht über die Āvaśyaka-Literatur, ed. by Walther Schubring (=Alt- und Neu- Indische Studien 4, Hamburg 1934). Since Alsdorf's lectures, a fresh start of that undertaking has been made: cp. Klaus Bruhn, Āvaśyaka Studies I (Studien zum Jainismus und Buddhismus, Gedenkschrift für Ludwig Alsdorf, Wiesbaden 1981, pp. 11-49).
29. Two Ph.D. dissertations dealing with this matter were written under Alsdorf's guidance subsequently: (i) Kiyoaki Okuda, Eine Digambara-Dogmatik — Das fünfte Kapitel von Vaṭṭakeras Mūlācāra, herausgegeben, übersetzt und kommentiert (=Alt- und Neu-Indische Studien 15, Wiesbaden 1975); (ii) Karl Oetjens, Śivāryas Mūlārādhanā — Ein Beitrag zur Kenntnis der Sterbefasten-Literatur der Jainas, Hamburg 1976.
30. Bibl. No. 33.

from the Aṇuogadārā (suttas 13 and 16) and the Uttarajjhāyā nijjutti (beginning), treating two terms of primary character, namely āvaśyaka and uttara.[31] At last, Alsdorf discussed the nature and mutual relation of the four kinds of exegetical Jaina texts (niryuktis, bhāṣyas, cūrṇis, and ṭikās) in his contribution to "Mahāvīra and His Teachings" in 1977.[32] He also substantiated the importance of the Āvaśyaka commentaries, promising further treatment of these texts — a remark to be understood as a challenge for the present generation.

31. Bibl. No. 34.
32. Bibl. No. 161.

Prof. K. R. Norman (Cambridge)

LUDWIG ALSDORF AND AŚOKAN STUDIES

LUDWIG ALSDORF's first major contribution to the field of Aśokan studies was an examination of the three versions of the so-called 'Schism Edict' in 1959.[1] The method he used was one which he was to use again in the future. In his belief that all three versions were intended to convey the same message, he used one to emend and correct the others. Since the word *lahiye* was legible in one, he assumed that the syllable *-yā/-ye* visible in the others stood for the same word, rather than *sakiye* as suggested by other scholars, and he gave evidence that *labhiye* with a negative could have the force of a prohibition. This enabled him to produce a translation 'There should not be schism in the Order' for all three versions. He then went on, as others had done before him, to relate this edict to the references in the Sinhalese chronicles to Aśoka's connection with the Third Council.

Alsdorf turned again to the subject of the Aśokan inscriptions in a contribution he made to a conference in 1959.[2] After a brief survey of the advances made in Aśokan studies since Hultzsch's edition of the inscriptions appeared in 1925, he laid particular emphasis upon the fragment of Rock Edict IX found at Sopārā in 1956, and the Aramaic-Greek bilingual edict which had been discovered at Kandahar in Afghanistan in 1958, and he suggested a number of parallels between phrases in the Greek version and Prakrit phrases from other edicts.

In a wide-ranging paper published in 1960,[3] Alsdorf discussed a variety of problems. After producing an edition of the new fragment from Sopārā, he proceeded to consider the relative authority of the different versions of the Rock Edicts, and drew attention to Lüders' view, which had been rather overlooked by later scholars, that the Girnār version, so far from holding the foremost position allotted to it by many, was in fact the least authoritative

1. Bibl. No. 44.
2. Bibl. No. 46.
3. Bibl. No. 45.

of all the versions, and not infrequently mistranslated the Eastern original of the Rock Edicts. Other points discussed in this paper similarly emphasised the fact that the Eastern versions are closer to Aśoka's original than the Western and North-Western ones, and Alsdorf gave convincing proof that in at least one passage an error in a Kharoṣṭhī version must be assumed to go back to an underlying Brāhmī version, with important repercussions for the way in which the edicts must be assumed to have been distributed and promulgated. One of the most important items in this article was the investigation of the view put forward by M.A. Mehendale that the Separate Edicts found at Dhauli and Jaugaḍa had first been issued in the North-West, and still retained North-Western features which had been left by negligent translators. Every point put forward by Mehendale in support of his theory was subjected to a close scrutiny, as a result of which Alsdorf showed clearly that the suggestion was untenable.

The Separate Edicts were the subject of Alsdorf's next study. In 1962[4] he published a monograph in which he showed that the discrepancies between the two versions were by no means as great as had been thought, and could for the most part be explained away as wrong readings and scribal errors. As one reviewer of this work stated, 'His main originality lies in the masterly interpretations. Some of these become so clear and obvious, once he has explained them, and fit into the context so naturally that the previous interpretations appear far-fetched'.

Alsdorf's last contribution to the study of the Aśokan inscriptions was made in 1968,[5] when he returned to a subject which he had touched on earlier in the 1960 article, viz. the last few sentences of Rock Edict XIII. He was able to show conclusively, with the aid of the recently published Yerraguḍi version of the edicts, that the reference to a 'new victory' in this edict had been misunderstood by previous editors, while the reference to 'exertion' (*uyāma-*) in the Kālsī version of this edict was an invention of the scribe, based upon an error in the transmission of the edict.

How should we assess Alsdorf's contribution to the field of Aśokan studies? He deserves credit for three things. In the first place he reminded us of what Lüders had said many years before about the relative merits of the different versions. Probably because

4. Bibl. No. 11.
5. Bibl. No. 47.

he wrote in German, Lüders' views had been overlooked, particularly by Indian scholars but by European scholars also, and an undue emphasis was undoubtedly being placed upon the version at Girnār. Secondly Alsdorf reminded us that we must go back to the original inscriptions if we want to know what they say, and we must rely upon editions, for it frequently happens that when there is doubt about a reading, an editor sees only the reading which he wishes to see. Thirdly he showed us that a comparative study of all the versions of a particular inscription is the only way in which we are likely to get results.

Despite the importance of these contributions, it is likely that the impact of Alsdorf's writings will not be as great as it deserves to be, for despite his ability to write in almost flawless English, he followed his teacher Lüders in writing the greater part of his articles about the Aśokan inscriptions in German, which puts them out of the reach of many of those working in this field. To the extent to which many of his suggestions have been accepted by others and repeated in English, then they will be more widely known, but not necessarily as being made by him.

Not all, of course, of his views have been accepted. Some were merely suggestions, which could not be taken up without further evidence, which has not always been forthcoming. Against his suggestion of a connection between the 'Schism Edict' and the Third Council, it must be objected that the evidence of the inscriptions substantiates part of the tradition but not the whole. Since the edict makes no mention of the Council, it cannot be used as evidence that the Sinhalese tradition is correct. Nor, since it makes no mention of the cause of the schism, is it certain without further evidence that the schism to which it refers was in fact that mentioned in the Sinhalese chronicles.

Other suggestions which Alsdorf made were alternatives to already existing views, which they have not always supplanted. Some of his views were simply mistaken. The sum total of his writings, however, represents a very positive and considerable contribution to the field of Aśokan studies.

Prof. K. R. NORMAN (Cambridge)

LUDWIG ALSDORF AND PĀLI STUDIES

LUDWIG ALSDORF's first major work in the field of Pāli sutdies was a long and very valuable article on the Vessantara-jātaka, published in 1957.[1] The Vessantara-jātaka is the longest and best known of the Pāli Jātaka collection, but it bristles with difficulties. Alsdorf was able to suggest many emendations to the text, and also to show that the order of the verses was sometimes incorrect. He also pointed out that some of the verses were borrowed from the Cariyā-piṭaka, and that when these were removed the only unmistakably Buddhist verses in the text disappeared. His view was that the verses, the kernel of the story, were 'completely non-Buddhist'.

Alsdorf returned to his belief that some Pāli texts were un-Buddhist in origin in other writings. In a short contribution to the Horner Festschrift in 1974[2], he showed brilliantly how by comparing two very corrupt versions of the Chavaka-jātaka found in different parts of the Canon it was possible to restore the original version of this pre-, or at any rate non-, Buddhist anti-brahmanical poem. His last major work in the Pāli field, published in 1977[3], was a study of another anti-brahmanical Jātaka. By using the metre as a criterion, he was able to separate out an earlier stratum of the Nāga-story in Triṣṭubh metre found in the Bhūridatta-jātaka. This portion he re-edited and translated. By making use of oriental editions he was able, in a number of passages, to improve upon the readings found in Fausböll's edition, and thus solve many, if not all, of the problems which are found in this old text.

He had earlier made use of the same technique of distinguishing between an older and a younger portion of a Jātaka story in his examination of the Sivi-jātaka in 1968[4], when he succeeded in

1. Bibl. No. 36.
2. Bibl. No. 155.
3. Bibl. No. 158.
4. Bibl. No. 40.

differentiating between a Śloka version of the story and also a Triṣṭubh/Jagatī version. He was also able to do the same for the Vidhurapaṇḍita-jātaka in 1971[5], when his analysis showed that about half that text was in the Śloka metre. Most of this portion represented additions to an earlier core composed in the Vaitālīya and Triṣṭubh metres.

Alsdorf returned again and again to the study of the Jātaka collection, which he wrote of as being 'a treasure of the oldest folk poetry of India', and he was particularly interested in the stories which occur in both the Buddhist and the Jain traditions. In his studies of the 12th[6], 13th[7], and 25th[8] chapters of the Jain Uttarajjhāyā, he was able to combine together both his interest in Jain literature and his love for the Jātakas, and he showed convincingly that the hopes of earlier scholars to piece together the original versions of these stories by comparing their forms in the two traditions could not at present be fulfilled. The task was much more difficult than they had thought because whatever old poem underlay the two versions of each text had been so worked over by the Buddhist and Jain redactors that it was all but impossible to detect the original beneath all the alternations, additions, and omissions they had introduced.

Although many, perhaps the majority, of Alsdorf's publications in the field of Pāli studies were concerned with complete literary texts, nevertheless he was just as much at home in detailed philological studies of individual words and phrases. One of his earliest articles, published in 1959[9], was concerned with the stock phrase *sahadhammiko vādânuvādo gārayhaṃ ṭhānaṃ āgacchati*. By a meticulous comparison of all the passages where the phrase occurred, he was able to show where earlier editors and translators had gone astray in their interpretations.

Another detailed study of a single word is found in the article which he devoted to the Śaśa-jātaka and kindred texts in 1961.[10] Apart from the comparisons with Prakrit texts mentioned above, Alsdorf rarely moved outside Sanskrit and Pāli in his Buddhist

5. Bibl. No. 42.
6. Bibl. No. 32.
7. Bibl. No. 29.
8. Bibl. No. 32.
9. Bibl. No. 37.
10. Bibl. No. 38.

studies, and in view of the large amount of Buddhist source material available in Chinese and Tibetan, it is possible to regard his work as being, in consequence, somewhat restricted and one-sided. One of the very few occasions when he did venture further afield was in this study of the Śaśa-jātaka and Śaśāvadāna, which he concluded by comparing the Tibetan and Sanskrit versions of a portion of the Śaśāvadāna with a corresponding vagga in the Pāli Saṃyutta-nikāya. As a result of this, he was able to throw light upon the meaning of the compound *kalyāṇa-mitta*.

The greater part of Alsdorf's work in the philological field is to be found in his contributions to the Critical Pāli Dictionary. This is also the part which is likely to have the most effect, because it is in English and will be referred to by more readers than can read his literary studies, which are written almost entirely in German. Ironically, it is just this portion of his work which it is impossible to define accurately. With the exception of the two portions of the Dictionary which are expressly ascribed to him in fascicles 1 (1960)[11] and 5 (1968)[12] of Volume II, there is no way of assessing how much is directly due to Alsdorf in the fascicles produced under his editorship, and particularly in fascicles 8[13], 9[14], and 10[15], for which he prepared the typescript, in whole or in part, for the press. One small hint about the material which is concealed under this uninformative phrase is given by the article he published in 1975[16], entitled 'Pāli Miscellanies: uddhaṃsarā'. In this he gives a masterly explanation of the word *uddhaṃsarā*, upon which the article upon that word in fascicle 9 (published in the same year) is clearly based, although no reference is made to it.

The same article contains a penetrating study of the development of the Pāli prefix *ū-*, which is found before roots apparently beginning with *h-*, from the prefixes *ud-* and *upa-*. The suggestions made in that article will undoubtedly be enshrined in due course in the pages of the Critical Pāli Dictionary, and will thereby reach a far wider range of readers than the original article could ever do.

11. A Critical Pāli Dictionary. Begun by V. Trenckner, Vol. II, Fascicle 1. The Royal Danish Academy of Sciences and Letters, Copenhagen 1960. *āga — ā-gotrabhūto*.
12. op. cit., Vol. II, Fascicle 5, Copenhagen 1968. *āvi — Āvopupphiya*.
13. Copenhagen 1973.
14. Copenhagen 1975.
15. Copenhagen 1979.
16. Bibl. No. 156.